AMBITION
IN MINISTRY

Ambition IN Ministry

Our Spiritual Struggle with Success, Achievement, and Competition

ROBERT SCHNASE

Abingdon Press
Nashville

AMBITION IN MINISTRY:
OUR SPIRITUAL STRUGGLE WITH SUCCESS,
ACHIEVEMENT, AND COMPETITION

Library of Congress Cataloging-in-Publication Data

Schnase, Robert C., 1957–
    Ambition in ministry: our spiritual struggle with success, achievement, and competition/Robert Schnase.
        p. cm.
    ISBN 0-687-30144-0 (alk. paper)
    1. Clergy—Religious life. 2. Clergy—Psychology. 3. Ambition.
I. Title.
BV4011.6.S36   1993
248.8'92—dc20   92-38155

Scripture quotations are from the New Revised Standard Version Bible, Copyright 1989 by the Division of Christian Education of the National Council of the Churches of Christ in the U.S.A. Used by permission.

MANUFACTURED IN THE UNITED STATES OF AMERICA

Contents

Acknowledgments
7

CHAPTER 1

Achievement and Appetite
The Blessing and Curse of Ambition
9

CHAPTER 2

Individualism and Competition
The Sources of Ambition
22

CHAPTER 3

Ardent Desires and Deadly Appetites
Ambition Misdirected
42

CHAPTER 4

Bodies and Bucks
The Struggle for Integrity
62

CHAPTER 5

Influence Peddlers and Mathematical Magicians
The Politics of Ministry
79

CHAPTER 6

Accountable and Complete
The Gift of Living for Others
100

Epilogue
Always Excelling . . .
120

Notes
126

Acknowledgments

While browsing through the tape library at Princeton Theological Seminary, I came upon a short talk titled, "Should a Minister Be Ambitious?" Dr. George Sweazey's thirty minutes of reflection planted in my mind many seeds. This book is one of the fruits.

Each of us has our own personal church—those few folks whose friendship brings Christ's comfort and correction. I wish to thank Greg Hackett, Ken Harrison, Bill Hughes, Warren Hornung, Chuck McCullough, and Barrett Renfro. My preoccupation with the manuscript has meant that some of my daily responsibilities have slipped too much upon J'Nevelyn Lloyd and Brad DeHaven. I thank them for understanding.

Paul Franklyn's patience, friendship, and editorial insight have kept me on task, and for this I am thankful. My appreciation to First United Methodist Church in McAllen, Texas, for viewing writing as part of my ministry and for allowing me time to do it. Thanks too, to Calvin and Marge Bentsen for providing La Coma Ranch for refuge and concentration.

With love and affection, I dedicate this book to Esther. Through her encouragement, support, correction, and constant love, she has given me the strength and patience to write. I thank her, along with Karl and Paul, for allowing me the time I have needed.

Robert Schnase

CHAPTER ONE

Achievement and Appetite

The Blessing and Curse of Ambition

J oe had nurtured the dream of serving City Church for at least five years. He fantasized about preaching from the high, dark-wood pulpit in the beautiful sanctuary. Whenever he met staff members from City Church, he imagined what it would be like to work with them. He attended workshops on church growth—not just to sharpen his skills for his present church, but to prepare for an opportunity like City Church. City Church was not huge, but it held a place of special prominence. It offered an excellent salary, the highest among pastors in the area. And it had a certain prestige—everything seemed to revolve around City Church in Joe's mind.

When he heard that the present pastor was planning to retire, Joe talked to his supervisors and those entrusted with pastoral placement. He explained his interest in City Church, described his experience and strengths, and tailored his resume to accentuate the match between his talents and the church's needs.

Joe's wife never had shared his enthusiasm to the same degree. She would need to give up her excellent job and take the children out of the school system they liked. And she feared what the pressure might do to Joe. On other hand, the more Joe talked about City Church, the more she feared what might happen to him if he did not get it.

And now that day had arrived. The list of candidates for City Church had been narrowed to two, and Joe was not one of them. He felt the pain of disappointment twist through his soul.

The news was made even more difficult when he heard the names of the final two candidates. The first was the most ambitious, self-serving, manipulative pastor in the area, whom Joe had resented for years. Now indignation welled up with new ferocity. And he resented a placement system that would consider advancing such a person.

The second candidate evoked a different mix of emotions. This pastor was a solid choice, an excellent administrator, a gifted and challenging preacher who had done outstanding work in several churches. This person was more difficult to resent, but still Joe felt envious.

As Joe contemplated the two candidates and his feelings toward them, he wondered what other pastors felt about him. Was he viewed as ambitious and self-seeking? His interest in City Church had long been widely known. Or did his peers see him as qualified and appropriately assertive?

Now what? Joe sighed at the prospect of settling back into his present church. Somehow his ministry here seemed lackluster compared to his fantasies of City Church. He felt guilty about his neglect of his present responsibilities while he had poured all his energy into his hopes for advancement. He wondered where he would find the strength to re-engage. Only after he heard the disappointing news did Joe realize how focused his ambitions were toward City Church.

Ambition

The dictionary defines ambition as "the ardent desire to high position or to attain rank, influence, distinction." The picture drawn by these words is not altogether positive. *Ardent* sounds overheated, intense beyond reasonableness. Neither do *high position* and *rank* seem the loftiest of human strivings. The words tilt toward self-seeking. The definition rings the first warning bell.

But the word *ambition* casts a wider net. We do not use the word simply to define empty and selfish strivings. One's highest ambition may be to alleviate suffering or to produce the most perfect performance by a master composer. When General Booth founded the Salvation Army, he plunged into the slums of London motivated by "the impulses and the urgings of an undying . . . ambition."[1] Ardent, perhaps. But Booth hardly did what he did just to attain rank, notwithstanding his title.

To account for the positive and lofty strivings that have motivated the founders of schools, hospitals, and churches, that have led to great discoveries and brilliant masterpieces, Joseph Epstein has amended the definition of ambition as "the fuel of achievement."[2] Ambition is the passion for excellence and the striving for improvement that moves civilization forward. It releases the energies that propel us to fulfill our dreams.

Which are we to trust? Ambition sounds like the train we ought to take. On the other hand, we are warned about troubles on the track and almost certain derailment.

Ambitious Pastors

Our ambivalence about ambition is accentuated when we consider its place in the ministry. Ambition and ministry seem to be opposites. Ambition evokes images of a hard-driving person bent on accomplishing his or her own wishes. Ministry carries the connotation of one who serves, who seeks to help others meet their needs. Those in ministry may be tempted to believe that having ambitions could be a denial of their calling.

Jesus' teachings about humility and his warning against doing things in order to be seen by others make us suspicious of striving in almost any form. We may genuinely congratulate professors, bankers, and corporate workers in our congregation who do excellent work, aspire to higher positions, offer themselves for consideration, and receive promotions. We are happy for them when they seek and are named to important boards in their profession. But we feel awkward about pastors who strive for similar goals.

Because of this discomfort, most pastors conceal any stirrings of ambition. Pastors who admit to ambition threaten us. We consider them either ethically derelict or neurotic about their work. Consider these elements of ambition in pastors:

1. Ambitious pastors take the initiative. They seize opportunities, rather than passively waiting for things to happen. In the church, in the community, and in their careers, they actively influence outcomes. They energetically engage the world with their gifts and capacities, even at the risk of failure. At best, taking the initiative means they imaginatively and enthusiastically give all they have in service to God. At worst, it involves frantic efforts to impose their will on the world.

2. Ambitious pastors are achievement-driven. They look for ways to mark their progress; they seek outward measurable results for their efforts. This makes some pastors keenly aware of salary, church numbers, or awards, as they desperately search for evidence that they are progressing toward personal goals. Others search for evidence of lives changed, and thrive on a sense of having made a difference.

3. Ambitious pastors are future-oriented. A vision of possibilities ahead drives them. The next sermon, the next program, the next new member holds all the promise. At worst, they look down the road to calculate every consequence to themselves, motivated by the next promotion. At best, they are motivated by a hopeful vision of what the church should become, of the deepening spiritual life and extension of community blessings, pouring themselves into work to fulfill the vision.

4. Ambitious pastors have insatiable appetites. We do not view the person who sets a goal, reaches it, and enjoys satisfaction as ambitious in the same way we view the person who reaches goals but remains dissatisfied. Most positively, this means that ambitious pastors always have horizons to pursue, unfinished work that beckons, new projects that enliven their interests. The words *more,* and *higher,* and *deeper,* and *better* inspire them, whether this means doubling the attendance at Bible study or rising to the presidency of a club or pursuing an idea through a trail of books or polishing a sermon to brilliance. Negatively, this means that many pastors pursue receding goals and seldom enjoy the fruit of their effort before beginning other projects. Rather than

celebrating what they have attained, they look at what they have not attained and feel discouraged.

We perceive ambitious pastors as hurried, compelled to achieve their goals as soon as possible. We view the young pastor seeking to serve a 500-member church by age 28 as more ambitious than the young pastor who hopes to serve a 500-member church some day before retirement.

5. Ambitious pastors often display a competitive spirit. They derive energy from comparing their results to their own previous accomplishments or to the results of other pastors. At worst, this means that they can enjoy accomplishment only when their achievements are undergirded with a feeling of victory over someone else. At best, competitive elements are directed inward, driving pastors to surpass their own past performance.

6. Sometimes we perceive ambitious pastors as single-minded, intensely and persistently dedicated to a particular cause. When the concern is to improve a situation or to extend the church's ministry, we appreciate their dexterity with the issues and their energetic pursuit of action. When the cause they pursue relentlessly is their own advancement, we deplore their sagacity. Some characteristics of ambitious pastors do not reflect the positive elements of ambition, but rather the corruption of ambition.

Sometimes we deride ambitious pastors as people we shouldn't trust, those who willingly overstep moral boundaries to pursue their aims, who by definition are self-serving, avaricious, rapacious, and acquisitive. They seek only wealth and privilege and power. We narrow our definition of ambition to those who have no depth, exercise no sympathy, practice no introspection, display no imagination. They are "doers" and "go-getters," extraverting themselves onto every stage, without the counterbalance of thoughtfulness, prudence, and reflection.

Positive Ambition

Ambition's most fundamental characteristic is the energy of the soul that propels us to use ourselves to the fullest. It is our yearning to be, to do, to become. Ambition is what causes us to step forward into life rather than retreat, to lean into the future rather than withdraw. Our fundamental need to make a positive difference, to expand into our environment, to engage others and take up new challenges—all this comes from the stirrings of ambition in our souls.

Ambition gives color to our dreams and places before us an appetite for the possibilities of life. Ambition gives us the strength of character to turn aspirations into reality through muscle and sweat, mind and imagination. In its most subtle form, ambition is a feeling of restlessness with the status quo, being unsettled about the conditions of the world or agitated with the limits of one's own mind and work. More robustly, ambition fuels our dreams with an eagerness and a drive to accomplish with excellence whatever we set out to do.

Pastors work self-directed schedules. We answer to no immediate supervisor each day, and we punch no time clocks. Faithfulness to our call causes us to prepare sermons and visit hospitals and teach Bible studies. We can easily slip to the minimum requirements for the job.

Ambition drives us to excel above the minimum. It provides the extra effort to polish the sermon for the third and fourth time, to rise early to read over our Sunday school lesson once more, to add another program to a crowded church schedule, to assiduously follow the progress of our members through illness and grief. It gives us the vivid incentives, the eagerness to do our best and use ourselves to the fullest. When Christ invites us to preach and teach and heal and feed, and when our church ordains us to baptize and bury, to marry and counsel and visit, they expect us to do these things as well as we possibly can. The church never intended to provide pastors with just a way to make a living; it expects them to provide all Christians with the opportunity to develop and express a rich and varied assortment of inherent capabilities.

The cathedrals of the past, the monasteries that kept our faith alive during periods of darkness, the expansion of our churches into isolated communities, the founding of children's homes, the struggle for justice, the building of the churches we serve, the formation of the seminaries at which we learn, and the writing of the books we read—all find their genesis in the ambitions of Christians committed to influencing the world for Christ's purposes. When we dream and strive and toil to do better and to do more because of "the impulses and urgings of an undying ambition," God hallows and uses our ambitions.

Without ambition, we turn inward and live in ourselves. We fail to project our souls into the world. When we deny the energies to grow, we risk becoming untrue to ourselves and to God.

Destructive Ambition

Lest we soar too far, crowning ambition with too high an exultation, we must remember that any raw energy can be used either for good or for evil. The same force that propels us to great accomplishment can drive us headlong into destruction. Many of the most painful personal tragedies in pastoral ministry result from corrupted ambitions. The energies of the soul are so easily misdirected.

Pastors can allow society to provide the channels through which our self-expansive impulses flow, replacing the lofty ambitions of the gospel with the personal ambitions of money, prestige, position, and power. Such empty and self-centered ambitions have us panting after position rather than striving for great contribution. Usefulness for God in the world fades to obscurity behind pursuit of promotion. Such lowering of goals and narrowing of vision bring a torrent of negative and deadly results for pastors and churches alike. Consider ambition's many victims in the church:

1. Hard-driving, workaholic pastors are relentless in their strivings and can never stop to rest. Feverishly driven, sometimes toward ill-defined and unachievable goals, they risk marriage, home life, and their own mental well-being in the fervent pursuit of success and accomplishment. Seduced by the insatiability of ambition, they run full speed until they faint with exhaustion.

2. Some pastors sustain ambitions out of proportion to their abilities as they strive to fulfill responsibilities beyond their capacity. They yearn for churches they could never serve well.

By setting illusory goals, they guarantee themselves a painful fall. Either they acquire the churches they want and fail miserably, or they do not acquire them and feel cheated and frustrated. Their ambitions lead them into water too deep to get a footing. Propelled beyond their competencies, they live with chronic unhappiness and a disillusioning sense of failure. Many pastors languish in despair for the remainder of their careers after facing supervisors unwilling to "promote" them. Rather than questioning their expectations and ambitions, they question their own adequacy.

3. Some pastors fulfill their callings with excellence but feel painfully discouraged by a lack of the distinction and recognition they desire. Guilty for craving honor and distressed by its absence, their souls are darkened with despair.

Many satisfied and competent pastors who do outstanding work in 150-member churches now notice that fifteen years out of seminary, some of their colleagues serve 800-member churches and make double their salary. They feel they are in the right place, doing the right work, and yet they also feel left behind. At least part of their ambition remains unfulfilled.

Some pastors feel like failures because they had assumed that they would always move progressively upward toward more salary and bigger churches. The knowledge that it is statistically impossible for all pastors to serve larger churches, given the ratio of small churches to large, offers no consolation. We speak regretfully about pastors who make lateral moves, and moves toward lesser salary or responsibility crush the spirit. Even though it may make an unnoticeable difference in life-style or comfort, our ambitions make such steps backward an emotional catastrophe. We feel famished when we hanker for more but receive something less.

Ambition makes some pastors feel painfully under-utilized, serving churches that cannot absorb all their energies. They exercise excellent competencies, but feel frustrated and overlooked.

4. Ambition makes some pastors heedless of the competing claims of other clergy. Unharnessed personal ambition will shatter cooperative and covenantal relationships. After re-

alizing that other clergy are all that stand between them and the church they wish to serve, they perceive such pastors as obstacles to their happiness. Their ambition isolates them, and the ulcerous gnawing of competition eats away at their spirit.

As the cause of their ailment, spiritually depleted pastors often point to unfulfilled ambition, coupled with guilt about ambitious desires. Seven days a week, bankers can say that their goal is to make money. Clergy certainly are concerned about money, but on Sunday morning they may preach about it as an unworthy goal. Their families grieve over the inconsistency.

5. Ambition makes some pastors squirm with an endless itchiness for other possibilities. They no more than arrive at a new responsibility than they raise their heads from their own plowing to look for fields that hold more promise. They move at every opportunity that provides the slightest advancement. Their families pay the price in frequent relocation, in pursuit of larger churches and higher salaries.

6. Pastors can victimize churches through their personal ambitions. Congregations suffer when their pastors endlessly turn their hearts toward greater opportunities. Some churches perceive themselves as mere stepping stones for their pastors' career aspirations. When pastors are more concerned about their record of accomplishments than about the health of the church, the people of God intuitively know it.

Denominational processes also are victims of pastoral ambition. Sometimes denominations maintain bureaucratic positions far beyond their usefulness, merely to satiate the ambitions of those who hold, or desire to hold, the position and the prestige. Ambition shapes salary systems and ministerial deployment processes, as pastors strive for places of prominence and compete for high salaries. Ambition skews our view of success, lifting external evidences of achievement and measurable progress above many of the primary tasks of ministry.

And the most important victim of misdirected ambition is the gospel message. Pastors corrupt their ambitions when they compromise the gospel message or hedge on its truths in order to gain the approval and support they need to pursue their personal goals. When they present the gift of God's grace without the demands of God's grace, merely to add new members and improve the records; or when they offer quick fixes to churches instead of working at foundational change; or when they sacrifice community by engaging in ugly competition with other clergy, then ambitions undermine the faith.

Should Pastors be Ambitious?

Ambition drives pastors toward excellence in ministry. It also fosters fierce competition, unhappiness, disillusionment, and isolation. Ambition causes us to maximize our work, transform churches, and bring people to Christ. It also propels us toward destruction of community life. Without ambition among its pastors, the church withers and dies. On the other hand, pastors engulfed by ambition kill our most vital witness.

Most pastors would not want their peers to describe them as ambitious. They might appreciate being called energetic, hard-working, effective, or competent, but ambitious stirrings are downplayed, forbidden, hidden from public view.

On the other hand, most pastors would not enjoy being described as unambitious. The word brings to mind laziness and ineffectiveness.

We display a crippling ambivalence about ambition in the church.[3] We identify it as a source of clergy morale problems and misguided motivations. On the other hand, we say that the church needs more pastors who enthusiastically dive into the hard work of ministry—expanding programs, building new churches, reaching more people. Pastors who preach a meaningful message for 100 people should feel no embarrassment for yearning to preach the same message for 200. Anyone who has enjoyed the accomplishment of a job well done, the completion of a work of beauty, the achievement of a just cause, knows that ambition is not all bad.

Our ambiguity about ambition reaches our spiritual roots. Jesus warns against our pursuit for prideful place. He redirects the selfish ambitions of his disciples who seek to be first and greatest, and he restrains their acquisitiveness for power, prestige, and wealth. On the other hand, Jesus teaches the parable of the talents, which lifts high our responsibility to use our lives and our gifts to the fullest. Virtually every church reformer has burned with unquenchable ambition for the gospel, and yet our forebears of the faith named *ambition* as a shadowy cousin to the seven deadly sins.

In this book, we draw some distinctions, both ethical and spiritual. There are ambitions which we should accept and nurture and direct in our calling. But there are others that we should see as temptations to be wrestled with, dark undercurrents that we should condemn, restrain, and seek to overcome. Since ambition is ethically neutral in its origins, we will sort through the external pressures and internal impulses that transform healthy ambitions into destructive compulsions. We will acknowledge the objects of ambition and identify which ambitions can constrain and compress the human spirit.

The chapters that follow describe the inner dynamics which drive us toward achievement, and the pressures of our culture which channel our ambitions toward unhealthy objects empty of spiritual value. We reflect upon the internal forces that misdirect our ambitions—the spiritual hazards of pride, envy, greed, and anger. We consider the intransigence of the spirit which keeps us from leaning into life and ministry with all our strength and mind and spirit. A chapter on the politics of ministry describes ambition in the community of clergy. We explore the struggle for integrity that comes from our search for evidence of success in ministry. And finally, we propose ways to channel our ambitious impulses toward meaningful service so that mutuality in ministry will be enhanced.

The Identity of the Pastor

Reflection on ambition provides an arena for considering what it means to be a pastor in today's world.

Christ whispers motifs of self-sacrifice, while the culture blares strains of self-gratification. We hear both, and even though no one can serve two masters, most of us try. God and mammon seldom team up to give us everything we desire. We expound spiritual values while we covet material rewards. We want the best for our brothers and sisters in ministry, while we seek places of prominence and prestige for ourselves. We offer ourselves in genuine and humble service, at the same time aspiring for honor and recognition. Believing in love, sometimes we hate; valuing community, sometimes we compete in destructive ways. Self-giving impulses sometimes fade from view behind self-seeking appetites. We form our identities as pastors as we are pulled to and fro, rocked back and forth among these various external forces and internal impulses.

We face innumerable tensions as part of our calling. And among the difficulties with which we must cope is our unwillingness and inability to face the tension of our ambition honestly and redemptively.

There is a tension to this book that replicates the tension in our souls. We are suspended between genuine service and selfish appetites, between the role of servant bequeathed to us by our Lord and our culture's sense of success, between our need for community and our need for individual expression. And we never entirely resolve the tensions.

The book has grown from two convictions: first, that tension is an inescapable feature of ministry; and second, that from this tension can come life and growth.

When we accept tension on these terms, it helps us hold our call clearly in focus by keeping the question of servanthood freshly before us and the issues of integrity sharply in view. We are more likely to remain faithful by growing through the struggles—by using the tension to exercise our spirits and become stronger. When we lose sight of the tension by denying it or ignoring it, we miss the opportunity of growth it can stimulate and are more likely to fall into hazards we don't see coming. People aware of the possibility of getting lost will check the map more frequently and carefully, and so are more likely to stay on course than those blinded by their own confidence.

By granting the presence of tensions, by naming the dangers and confessing the temptations, we loosen their grasp on us and lessen their destructive impact.

This book is a journal for reflection. I wrestle with these issues, as do all conscientious pastors. This is my attempt to sort out for myself the influences upon me and the motivations within me, and to reflect upon the spiritual and theological commitment I have made as an ordained minister.

Together, let us sift through our motivations, or as Paul

requests of us, "Examine yourselves to see whether you are living in the faith" (II Cor. 13:5). Through faithful reflection, perhaps we can harness and redirect some of the more destructive aspects of ambition, restore a sense of genuine community among pastors, and free ourselves for more and greater work in Christ's service.

FOR PERSONAL REFLECTION OR GROUP DISCUSSION

◊

How important is it to a pastor's spiritual well-being to explore the issue of ambition? Why is ambition difficult to talk about among pastors? What other significant personal, relational, or professional issues are seldom discussed directly and openly? Why are these topics avoided? What setting makes exploration of these issues more redemptive for you?

◊

Is ambition a more pressing issue or a more dangerous hazard at some stages of ministry than at others? Why is ambition a source of unhappiness or divisiveness in ministry?

◊

How has ambition affected your achievement, effectiveness, and satisfaction positively? Negatively?

◊

How are the energies and risks of ambition for men different from those for women? For pastors, from those for other professionals?

◊

Can someone have too much ambition? Too little? What makes ambition healthy or unhealthy—the objects we pursue?; the intensity of our work?; our motivations?; the effect on relationships?

◊

Think about a pastor you admire deeply. How has ambition shaped her or his life? What place does the desire for advancement hold in that person's career satisfaction?

CHAPTER TWO

Individualism and Competition

The Sources of Ambition

Mother buckles the youngest in the front seat while Mark climbs into the back. But the older child has more on his mind than the routine trip to church school.

"How come Christi always gets to sit up there with you, but I can't? It's not fair."

Searching to calm the concern, Mother carefully explains, "Christi is younger than you and needs my help, but you're a big boy and can sit by yourself." But explanations to the mind do not relieve questions from the heart.

Younger sister, quite skilled at exploiting her brother's vulnerabilities, sees her opportunity and stings him: "Mommy loves me more."

"No she doesn't! You're just a baby!" brother responds.

"Yes she does! I get to sit in the front seat. She loves me better."

"Mommy, tell Christi that's not true. You love me more! I'm bigger!" Mark's words enlarge the wounds far beyond the significance of the occasion.

When mother turns to the back seat to bring the conversation to a close, she is stunned by the severity of her son's expression.

He clenches his fists and screams, "You love me more, Mommy. Tell Christi you love me best of all!" His watery eyes betray the bolstered confidence in his words, with the effect of bending the exclamation point into a wiry question mark.

Am I really loved at all? seems to be Mark's earnest concern through the whole ordeal.

In the Beginning

Early in this century, Freud shocked the world by describing the inner life of the child as a cauldron boiling with destructive sexual and violent impulses. His analysis sounds too severe, in light of our experience of the innocence of childhood. But Freud took more seriously than his predecessors the powerful drive toward self-interest and the fierce hostility that show up from the earliest years.

Alfred Adler tempered Freud's view somewhat, nevertheless contending that each of us is born with a will to power, a natural desire to overtake others, a delight in our own sense of superiority. According to Adler, all of us are born with a natural drive to have more and be more than those around us.

As brutal as these analyses sound, they resonate with some Christian notions about original sin. We are born with self-serving appetites, which, if unchecked, destroy us by denying us communion with God and with one another. We naturally acquiesce to the tragic tendency to set ourselves up as the center of everything, but God's grace remolds self-centered impulses so that we can enjoy fullness of life, as God intends.

Developmental psychologists elaborate a similar point, though without the censure of early theology or the severity of Freud and Adler. Children naturally go through an extensive period of egocentricity. Young children assert their own claims because they cannot possibly be aware of the claims of others. Children are naturally selfish, because their limited perceptual, intellectual, and social development makes them unaware of anything but themselves.

As children mature, they balance this natural egocentricity with an ability to reflect on the feelings of others and to consider the implications of their actions. When this mutuality fails to develop, children grow into adults with no reservations about using others for their own purposes.

All serious theologies and psychologies describe the inborn tenacity of our self-centeredness and our drive for power. The roots of ambition extend deeply, finding their source in the formation of human nature.

Who Will Be First?

As in the example that opens this chapter, young children place unlimited importance upon who receives the most ice cream, who goes to bed last, who gets to sit closest to Mom. Sibling rivalry begins the first day the second child arrives home from the hospital, and it foreshadows some of our struggles for self-affirmation that we carry late into life. Sibling rivalry offers an excellent analogy and a good choice of words for describing some of our conflicts with other pastors for positions of prominence.

Children look for clues to confirm that they matter. They harbor the suspicion that perhaps something else or someone else is at the center of the world rather than themselves. At the root of sibling rivalry is each child's deep desire for the *exclusive* love of his or her parents. The craving to be the one and only comes from the frightening thought that "if Mom and Dad are showing all that love and concern and enthusiasm for my brother and sister, maybe they're worth more than I am. And if they are worth more, that must mean that I'm worth less. And if I am worth less, then I'm in serious trouble." As Faber and Mazlish conclude, "No wonder children struggle so fiercely to be first or best. No wonder they mobilize all their energy to have more and most. Or better still, ALL. Security lies in having all of Mommy, all of Daddy, all the toys, all the food, all the space."[1]

In sibling rivalry, we catch an early glimpse of the relentless competitiveness and selfishness, at times all-absorbing, which reveals our yearning to be at the center of the universe. Our insatiable desire for affirmation brings to the surface our impulse to supersede.

Achieving for Approval

Self-esteem is the healthy self-regard that we need in order to feel positive about ourselves. It is the level of inner assurance we perceive when we reflect intuitively upon the question, "Am I worthwhile? Am I loved?"

As parents attach praise to some activities and disapproval to others, they communicate a connection between conduct and worth. Children have difficulty distinguishing between the value their parents place on their behaviors and the value their parents place on them as persons. "Punish the behavior but not the child" is a distinction few children can appreciate.

Despite their parents' best efforts at affirmation, children hear the message, "If you do this, I'm pleased, and you're loved." Even though parents strive to provide unconditional love, children may experience approval and love as conditional. The child accepts this formula as a blueprint for understanding the world and its people.

From "my parents love me for what I do," the child moves naturally to "I win love from others on the basis of my achievements." Reward systems sustain this reality in schools, sports, work, and the media.

As parental approval shapes appetites for love and self-validation, ambitions become achievement-oriented. But it is questionable whether children ever can *do* enough to sustain an adequate sense of self-esteem, and sometimes approval and love are not forthcoming despite their best efforts. The search for self-validation, when it finds its source and end in achievement, never rests secure.

Parents can abuse the connection between self-esteem and achievement. David Elkind writes extensively on childhood pressures to achieve. He sees "too much pressure to achieve, to succeed, to please, [and too great a] fear of failure."[2] Parents push children too fast, toward too many different kinds of achievement. Kids sense that love depends upon fulfilling the expectations of their parents, but the goals are too high and diverse to accomplish, shattering any hope of finding a sustainable level of self-esteem.

Competition

Schools need tools to motivate and evaluate the progress children make in their learning, and much of that evaluation is comparative and competitive. From grading systems to spelling contests, teachers emphasize doing better than the other children. The A's and B's sustain no sense of achievement unless somebody else makes C's and D's.

Our educational systems connect knowledge (what is learned) to grades (the tool of evaluation) to the reward (praise and pleasure from teacher and parents). It is the praise and pleasure that provide the sharpest motivation.

Productive life requires a healthy self-assertiveness; useful compulsiveness and adaptive competitiveness drive thousands through graduate school and beyond. If such evaluation inspires a desire for the best, an attention to detail, and an appreciation for excellence, then competition serves us well. Children who lack any desire to achieve are not emotionally healthy. Education requires a link between the child's natural impulse toward superiority and constructive goals. Then ambition comes alive in studies, sports, music, and invention, in productive and satisfying ways.

Schools foster self-expression and stoke the coals of a healthy ambition when they seek to bring out the best. But too much competition and comparison feeds selfish and hostile striving, which furthers isolation rather than fostering community. Television, movies, and advertising enhance comparison and competition during the early years and also help provide the objects toward which youngsters strive. The media highlight the best, the fastest, the strongest, the smartest, and the highest paid. Being good at something does not draw as much attention as being the best.

On the Job

The work world further binds self-worth to achievement. We connect knowledge, competence, and productivity to position and praise, and we tie all these to salary, authority, and power.

Under the influences of our culture, adults sometimes pursue salary and power as provocative ends in themselves. Salary and position symbolize our usefulness; they indicate how highly our corporation and society value our work and thus form the foundation of our sense of self-worth and purpose. Just as self-esteem is tied to grades and achievement in childhood, it is linked to rank and salary in adulthood.

But problems arise when we require our jobs and salaries to carry the burden of sustaining our sense of self-worth. "Whenever personal worth is dependent upon performance, personal value is subject to cancellation with every misstep."[3] When we fail to perform well, we fail as a person. We ask more from our jobs than they can possibly provide, seeking through them to achieve security and validation.

With self-validation derived from what we do in relation to others and measured in salary, we never can feel fully worthwhile. Even the person at the top feels on the lowest rung of the ladder, when compared with people in other careers or those with a different mixture of gifts.

Shaped by Culture

Pastoral aspirations are shaped by our culture's emphasis on individuality and competition; we are provided with a ready-made guide to the activities and measures for happiness. But when we overlay the old map of culture with the new map of the gospel, we can still see the roads underneath and easily confuse the paths we should travel.

When individualism colors our vision of ministry, we see pastors as self-reliant, independently functioning units, advancing their personal, essentially self-interested claims. We compete and risk and create for ourselves, and in the flurry of action and conflict that result, the church progresses, as competition brings out the best in all of us.

When individualistic impulses beat strong, ambitious pastors do not tie their futures and fortunes to the claims of community, but aim at rising above it, isolating and pursuing our rights and desires apart from community concerns.

Relations with others become a means to an end; we win friends in order to influence circumstances for our own goals.

Through the lenses of individualism, we see our conferences, dioceses, and presbyteries as collections of competing individuals, rather than as a unified force with all participating in the same vital work. We isolate our own work in our own church from the work others fulfill in theirs, seeing our contributions as discontinuous and almost unrelated. We draw distinct lines between our ministry and the work of our predecessors and successors, defending the boundaries with a good deal of emotional energy.

We live with the myth of the pastor who "goes it alone," saving churches and souls with a distant aloofness, then moving on to the next cry for help. Positive changes in local churches are described and experienced as personal victories for the pastors involved, rather than celebrated as attainments for the laity with whom we minister. Individualism creates in us the belief that our own choices and hard work should determine where we go next, with a minimum of outside interference. Our willingness for toil and tears, together with our capacity for ingenuity and leadership, provide the only limits to our ascendancy. We trust that a ministry can be built upon our own vision, without the corrective influence of supervisors or community.

Individualism weakens our inclination to share our work, our glory, our worries, or even ourselves. Unbalanced by community, it creates isolated pastors and fosters impersonality, mistrust, and antagonism, as we each shut ourselves up in the solitude of our own work. Ambitions are personalized, turned inward, and propel us away from one another. One of the most pressing and hidden issues in ministry is the stark loneliness of our pastors.

We claim that competition for higher salaries causes people to work harder; vying for key positions causes us to bring all our faculties to bear. We highlight individuals with growing churches to inspire others to pursue similar results, but competitive models inspire as much antagonism as excellence.

And therein lies the spiritual risk when pastors adopt productive competition as a paradigm for their relationships

with other pastors. Competition translates the joy of achievement into the thrill of victory. We find our happiness not in
doing *well*, but in doing *better* than another.

Such awards do influence productivity, but in the conflict of
values, we must decide whether productivity gained is worth
covenantal community lost. We must assess competition in
terms of the outcome in bringing the gospel to others and
enhancing the witness to the Kingdom.

Metaphors of Ascendancy

A subtle concept that shapes our thinking as pastors is the
spatial metaphor, "Up is good"[4]: "Things are really looking
up"; "She's on *top* of the world"; "He was *promoted*"; "She's
climbing the ladder"; "The cream always *rises*"; "He's *above*
me in salary"; "Let's *advance* him to a *bigger* church."

"Up" is good and "down" is bad. In a culture that values
individualism, the road to appropriate individuation follows
these metaphors of ascendancy. We come into our own as
individuals by moving up. Promotion, salary increases, rising
above others in a hierarchy—these define success, not only in
crude media caricatures but in the subtle regions of thought,
language, and value.

We evaluate career opportunities and churches under the
heavy influence of such factors. Does this church move me up?
and Will I have a bigger salary? may take precedence over
Does this church need what I can offer? When the most
compelling reason for moving to another church is a higher
salary, we have been seduced by culture.

If we break free of the "up is better" metaphor, we realize
that other questions should determine whether we make a
move. Maybe the operative question is not, Does this move me
up? but, Does this move me closer?—closer to the work God is
calling me to do. *Closer* is not as easy to measure as *up*. We
should understand *closer* in terms of the usefulness of our
talents in the new position, the satisfaction we find in our
work, the effect of a move on our families, and how much our
gifts are needed in the situation offered as compared to the
ministries underway in our present church.

Our premium on moving "up" makes some excellent preachers give up their preaching to work poorly as superintendents, and it causes some crackerjack pastors in 150-member churches to trade the satisfaction they enjoy for a sense of failure in 600-member churches. Because something is higher and bigger, we feel we cannot refuse.

Certainly there are times when the most conscientious response to the offer of larger responsibility is a positive and enthusiastic acceptance. But the unquestioned high premium we place on *big* and *more* and *up* may come from our internalized cultural voice, telling us we would be stupid to pass up such an opportunity. Each decision needs to be made prayerfully, without an automatic acquiescence to the cultural expectation of material advancement.

Unless we appeal to other values, our culture digs the channels through which our self-expansive energies flow. After James and John requested positions of honor for themselves, Jesus mixed all our metaphors and countered our cultural values by saying, "Whoever wishes to be great among you must be your servant" (Matt. 20:26*b*). He did not say, "Your ambitious feelings are wrong," but in effect, "Express your ambitions in a different way. Channel them into service."[5]

There are times when accepting a smaller church is the highest good. There are times when serving a church at reduced salary provides the richest opportunity to fulfill our ambitions.

Objects for Pursuit

Our society also provides a consensus of which objects of our ambitions are appropriate for individuation.

WEALTH—Society teaches that the rewards we receive correspond to the relative usefulness of our contribution, as compared to others. Salary is an objective sign of approval for producing measurable results.

Salary, comparative and competitive in most denominations, affects many pastors' sense of self-worth. For many, the question is not, Are my needs satisfied? but How am I doing as compared to others?

Sometimes we seem inordinately preoccupied with salaries. There's hardly a gathering of pastors that one of the following issues does not surface—how salary packages should be organized, tax short-cuts, travel allowances, reimbursement for expenses, minimum salaries, big-church salaries, cost-of-living increases, salary comparisons with other clergy and other professionals. We exert a tremendous amount of emotional energy in lamenting our lower salaries or defending our desire for higher salaries.

POWER—Our culture lifts up as heroes those with the capacity to control their destiny. When our work carries the colossal burden of justifying our existence, we seek symbols of our usefulness, including our power over others.

The campaigns for the episcopacy and the maneuvering to superintend ministry stokes the fires of many pastors' ambitions. Many times the actual work of superintending is unattractive and dull to those who covet such positions; it's the power and prestige that make holding such authority so enticing.

FAME—Our society places a high value on being known, recognized, looked up to, sought after, and remembered.

Pastors feel compelled by the image of the high-steeple preacher and hunger for the visibility of certain positions in our denominations. We put extra hours into our sermon preparation—not just to increase our effectiveness, but to nurture the dream that one day we may preach in a place of prominence.

PRESTIGE—The more people who covet a position, the more valuable it becomes. Our culture directs our ambitions toward owning things that are prestigious and holding prestigious jobs.

Sometimes we drive toward the center instead of climbing up the ladder. Many pastors seek certain positions because they are at the hub of activity, not because of the salary.

Pastors are as vulnerable as everyone else to the desire to join prestigious groups. The rich and powerful in our congregations provide seductive glimpses of life from the other side, and sometimes we go out of our way to join the status group. In our role as pastors, we enter luxurious homes we can never own and eat in country clubs we could never join. For some, these experiences cause a longing that can never be satisfied in the ministry.

Premium on Success

Success is simply the achievement of something we attempt, and our society pressures us to believe that we must achieve *everything* we attempt. In a cruel twist, we have come to believe that the only alternative to success is failure.[6] *Failure* once meant losing everything, falling completely into destruction and despair, but the word has been redefined as simply not achieving what we have set out to do. *Failure* now describes productive people of integrity who have not climbed to the top in their careers in the way they had hoped.

Our premium on success fosters the assumption that the natural course of life is one of unending achievement and advancement, that careers move without interruption from lower to higher positions of responsibility and compensation. Merely to hold one's place is stagnation, and to step back from any tangible sign of success (for example, to accept a reduced salary) is viewed as failure.

Crossroads

Paul writes, "Do not be conformed to this world, but be transformed by the renewing of your minds, so that you may discern what is the will of God" (Rom. 12:2).

The J. B. Phillips version translates this passage beautifully: "Don't let the world squeeze you into its mold." Culture threatens to do precisely this with our most genuine ambitions. By narrowing our definition of success, focusing our eyes only upon culturally approved objects, and bending our energies selfishly back upon ourselves, our culture compresses our spirits and limits our usefulness.

Every pastor negotiates the crossroads between Christ and culture. The intersection is a dizzying place to stand, since we bear witness to a cooperative spirit in a society that commends competition. As Americans, we can't help valuing a bigger house and a better car, while as Christians we know that the value of these things is illusory. We ask our lay people to sacrifice financially for Christ, while we seek pastorates with a maximum of financial advantage for ourselves. The more sensitive the pastor's spirit, the more difficult the task of discipleship.

According to C. G. Jung, "Achievements which society rewards are won at the cost of a diminution of personality."[7] The question for all pastors is whether we are willing to risk such imbalance by pursuing only the sliver of our capacities that is rewarded by society.

The Need for Community

The psychodynamic theories, the sibling rivalry, the need for self-validation, the achievements rewarded by our parents, the victories nourished by competition, the incentives of salary and position—all these shape our ambitions. But the most compelling way to understand the needs that fuel or inhibit our ambitions is to reflect on the pull between community and individuality. We forge our ambitions in the tension created by our need to be a part of community pulling against our yearning to stand out from community.

All of us have the internal need to pour our lives into something bigger than ourselves, to experience a sense of purpose through belonging to something more lasting, and to enjoy a special kinship with others. We need to be accepted, to work together, to find power and meaning through cooperation. We need to merge our lives with those of others.[8]

Aligning ourselves with others helps us to defend against a feeling of isolation and powerlessness. Those aspirations that we could not possibly achieve through an individual human life, we can achieve through a community of committed lives. We discover continuity with those before and those to follow.

The need for community drives people to heroic sacrifice and accounts for a myriad less ultimate commitments. Thousands in every generation lay down their lives for their countries in their loyalty to community. Athletes sacrifice to contribute their best to the team. The need to be a part of something bigger drives some people toward civic organizations and others into street gangs. Our search for significance binds us together in mutually dependent relationships—in the family, among our peers, in career associations, in our church, in our city, in our nation.

Our ministry enhances community life. We preach that we are dependent creatures, created for community. We teach that abundant life comes through loving and being loved, from sharing and offering ourselves to others.

The Yearning to Stand Out

In contrast, we also have a deep yearning to express our unique talents and abilities, to stand out from community. We have personal aspirations apart from community goals. We have the "urge for more life, for exciting experience, for the development of our self-powers, for developing the uniqueness of the individual creature, the impulse to stick out of nature and shine."[9]

Sometimes we feel that we limit our self-expression by submitting our purposes to the community; we sense that we can find our fullest potential only by striking out on our own. Community can swallow us up into insignificance if we do not develop our potential and expand our capacities. We need a sense of purpose apart from the group.

These two internal urges, toward community and toward individual expression, pull us in opposite directions. We can't stand the isolation that comes with asserting our individuality, but neither can we tolerate stifling our natural impulses toward self-expression. We have a "deep desire for autonomy and self-reliance combined with an equally deep conviction that life has no meaning unless shared with others in the context of community. . . . We need one another as much as we need to stand alone."[10]

Football players cheer for the other players on their team and want to win the championship. On the other hand, every football player dreams of scoring the game-winning touchdown. Every choir member experiences chills down the spine during the harmony and power of combined efforts. But choir members also covet the privilege of offering the key solo in the performance.

These two impulses are present in each of us at every gathering of pastors. When we join with our brothers and sisters to share the sacrament of communion at conferences or synods, we gain unspeakable strength from our time together. Pastors of all ages and races file past to receive the elements. The occasion becomes a review of our ministries, reminding us of the special relationships that formed us. We see pastors to whom we long have been indebted, and those with whom we have become acquainted only recently. There are the well-known pastors and the hardly recognized, those in retirement and others new from seminary.

Such experiences of community anchor our covenant to one another. They remind us of our ordinations, the mutual bonds we enjoy, our shared submission to the work of the church. Such times present to us the gift and demand of community. Communion services, ordination services, retirement services, clergy funerals—these are just a few of the pivotal moments in the community of pastors.

In contrast, when we gather with other pastors, we enjoy the privilege of chairing a committee, or presenting a new program, or leading our community in worship. We accept as a privilege the invitation to offer the keynote address at a training session. We covet being elected to high office by our colleagues. We find a sense of accomplishment in doing what we do best and offering our distinct capabilities. We enjoy having our own special projects headlined in the denominational newsletter. Seeing the local church we serve receive commendation for mission gives us a well-deserved sense of satisfaction and self-affirmation.

We are motivated to give ourselves to the community from which we find our purpose, and we also feel moved to stand out in that community by using our unique gifts. We want to be fully identified with the community, but we also want to be more than just one of the crowd.

The Essential Tension

We feel unfulfilled if we experience community without having individuality. Our yearnings for self-expression are frustrated.

But if we have individuality without experiencing community, we feel isolated from the most profound sense of community and guilty about our separation from others.

Tracy Kidder, a Pulitzer Prize-winning author, captures this tension superbly in his description of the top student in a fifth-grade class:

> Chris [the teacher] had noticed that praise made Judith shy. It had taken Chris a while to realize that was because Judith was even smart about being smart. When she got an A on a paper, which was usually, Judith put it away in her desk before her classmates could see it. Judith felt that her teachers had always praised her too openly. "I like the way I do good in school, but I don't like overpraising. It makes me feel like, like the other kids look at me like someone else."[11]

Feel the tension in those words! Judith wants to excel, to do her best, to use her talents to the fullest. But she knows that to outdistance the other students will leave her cut off. She feels that she needs to conceal her uniqueness so she can enjoy community with her classmates. She needs to do her best, but she needs friends, too.

When pastors receive a considerable promotion or attain an achievement of distinction, they experience a potent mixture of feelings. They enjoy a wonderful sense of self-affirmation. But their joy is often tempered by the responses of their colleagues—responses clouded by envy and resentment. As if an unexpected earthquake creates a great canyon among us, one pastor's success shakes the foundations of community. The sudden shift twists friendships and strains relationships. Sometimes the most joyous times of a career in ministry are the loneliest moments.

When Joseph Epstein defines ambition as the "fuel of achievement," he describes this individual desire to excel.[12] And Herman Melville calls ambition "the most secret of passions," because for it to be otherwise would risk loss of community.

The way a person forges a path through the tension between these two impulses will determine the quality of his or her life.[13] The challenge is to discover how to be an individual in community, and how the community can affirm individuality. As William James writes, "The community stagnates without the impulse of the individual. The impulse dies away without the sympathy of the community."[14]

Ambition expresses our natural need for individuation, a healthy and essential part of moving toward full personhood. It becomes destructive only when it thwarts our need for one another and constrains mutuality. To the extent that our yearning to stand out overpowers our need for community, we destroy part of ourselves and suppress the gift and grace of community. On the other hand, if community stifles self-expression, personhood is destroyed.

The solution lies in tempering our ambitions with a deeper sense of community and in transforming our community life so that it not only tolerates but fosters autonomous expression. The final test of healthy ambition is whether it drives us toward objects that promote the common good, while it uses our individual impulses to the fullest.

Unhealthy Forces

Unhealthy forces can also fuel ambition. Sometimes we ambitiously immerse ourselves in our work—not to attain some future goal, but to escape a painful past or avoid present tribulation. Our relentless industry so fills our mind and soul that we have no time to face issues about ourselves that we would prefer to avoid. Ambition covers our escape and helps us move farther away from self-understanding.

At one pastors' retreat, the leader asked, "What are you running from?" This question evoked many insightful and emotional responses. Some were running from a sense of failure; others from painful relationships. Some were fleeing from the reality that they may be average rather than outstanding, and others were seeking to escape a deep sense of loneliness.

We've all known pastors (and church members) who work tirelessly at their jobs and endlessly at their play and fruitfully in their churches—all in order to avoid evenings at home, untangling troubled family relationships. Industry is a socially acceptable escape mechanism.

Ambitious involvement in the world grants reprieve from pain. But ambition that causes us to shrink back from life instead of embracing it seldom leads to satisfying and productive work.

Feeling Like a Fraud

Sometimes we drive ourselves to excel in an attempt to compensate for feeling like a fraud. We do things well, but deep inside we feel that we are not as competent as others think we are. So we pour ourselves into extra work to overcome our sense of inadequacy. Our fear of weakness drives us.

Or we feel that people will discover that we are not as pure as they might think. All pastors who honestly sift through their motivations occasionally uncover cesspools of envy and animosity. The presence of such emotions makes us feel guilty and angry. We doubt our call, question our worthiness, and mistrust our abilities. Excessive work helps us to cover up such feelings.

Such fears and doubts begin a never-ending struggle with the suspicions of the mind, an enemy so elusive that we can never stand victorious. Seldom can we experience satisfaction from our achievements when they are motivated by fear of being found out.

Starving for Acceptance

Some ambitions come from our desperate need for love and acceptance. When we search to please others, we live in reflexive dialogue with the expectations of family, friends, church members, and strangers.

Instead of measuring ourselves by the highest values of our spiritual lives, we conform to the fleeting desires of those around us. We are not marching to the drumbeat of eternity, but merely responding to the clamor of the crowd. This is not genuine self-expansion, but simply a way to keep up with the standards of others. Self-worth based on the approval of others is revokable upon any infringement and can come shattering down in an instant.

When we look to our placement systems and supervisors to provide all our validation, absorb all our aspirations, and sustain all our affirmation, we ask more than they can possibly grant. Our dependency on them leaves us vulnerable to career crises and spiritual collapse.

Fear of Death

Sometimes we scream for glory when we confront our own mortality. We fear that if we don't do something worthwhile, our lives will count for nothing. If we do accomplish that something, we draw enough attention to extend our influence a little farther and be remembered a little longer. Ernest Becker writes extensively about death as the "mainspring of human activity"—our fear or denial of it drives us to works that will outlive us.[15]

The thought of people yet unborn feeling indebted to us gives us assurance about our accomplishments. But this view posits death as an enemy, robbing us of life if we do not achieve enough before it approaches. When we work because we are driven by fear, we contradict the Christian view that death cannot rob us of life.

What Are We Really After?

Through the intensity with which we rival others for our parents' love, through the grasping to be first and the best in school, through the fierce struggles of our work, what do we seek? When we seek self-validation by pursuing the expectations of others, or when we try to win the love of others, or try to embrace immortality through our works, what do we really want?

Redemption—nothing less! Whether by being part of community or rising above it, we want to banish our feelings of nothingness. We want to know that we have not been created in vain. We want validation for all that we are. We seek redemption from the terrible thought that in the endless immensity of space and the eternal span of time, we might live, work, love, and die for no notable purpose at all. We cry out from our depths for some evidence that we matter.

This chapter opened with the example of sibling rivalry. "Am I really loved at all?" was the child's deepest concern. From cradle to grave, we search for evidence of our worth. We offer our works and achievements, the products of our ambition, as paltry proof of our specialness.

But we cannot squeeze the infinite out of the temporal. Our work and creativity may bring satisfaction, but they never resolve all the questions of the soul or completely fill our need for meaning. We cannot find the eternal in things finite and deteriorating. We huddle over treasures that moth will eat and rust consume. Our final validation does not come from our achievements. In fact, it does not come from us at all.

The curious irony for ministers is that we can find the answer to our striving only in the message with which we have been entrusted.

FOR PERSONAL REFLECTION AND GROUP DISCUSSION

◇

What are some of your earliest memories of the satisfaction of achievement? What form did competition take in your family and education? Has competition played mostly a positive or a negative role in your life?

◇

How does a congregation foster competitive and individualistic impulses among children, youths, and adults? What denominational systems and practices encourage competition among pastors? How do you evaluate the role of competition in enhancing or diminishing faithfulness and effectiveness in ministry?

◇

How is a sense of community nurtured among pastors in your area? How does the community of pastors respond to individuals who attain achievements of distinction or express unusual innovation or effectiveness? Are these expressions welcomed and fostered, or downplayed and stifled?

◇

In the section on "Unhealthy Forces," the statement is made that industry is a socially acceptable escape mechanism. What does this mean? And how can excessive work help cover feelings of inadequacy or unworthiness? What is unhealthy about work produced under the influence of such motivations?

CHAPTER THREE

Ardent Desires and Deadly Appetites

Ambition Misdirected

Sometimes we are certain about where we stand and where we wish to go, but between point of departure and destination, we fail to take into consideration the crosswinds that cause us to veer off course. Like the pilot taken unaware by the ferocity of wind shears, or the swimmer who underestimates the persistence of riptides, we tragically end up somewhere other than where we intended to go. With miscalculation by a few degrees, the same ambitions that propel us toward great service and important contribution can thrust us into isolation and despair.

A pastor's soul rises and falls, steps forward and withdraws, under the influence of diverse yearnings and robust temptations. This chapter explores our secret inner terrain, the ambitions that fuel our journey, and the hazardous currents we dare not ignore.

For centuries, church thinkers have identified the temptations which invite internal corrosion and spiritual death. These deadly sins which echo from antiquity still resonate through the community life of pastors today and can cause us to step out of community and into isolation.

The early saints, in their efforts toward faithfulness, found such unwanted guests lodging in their own hearts and cluttering up their community life. These sins represent the ever-present undertow of the spiritual life, exhausting energies, impeding growth, threatening death. No pastor escapes seduction. Regardless of how genuine our intent or how clear our commitments, these tendencies skew our perspectives and redirect healthy ambitions toward unsavory ends.

Pride

Pride is the excessive preoccupation with our accomplishments, possessions, position, abilities, or honors. It is self-love gone too far, until it overshadows our love for others and even our love for God.

Consider the characteristics of pride. First, it makes us think too highly of ourselves, possessed by our own indispensability. Under pride's force, we sail away from reality, caught up in our own greatness, buffeted along to the land of delusion. A story is told of a bishop, driving away from a particularly successful preaching mission.

Feeling quite good about his pulpit presence, he asked his wife, "How many really *great* preachers do you think there are in Protestantism today?"

Without hesitation, his wife answered, "Exactly one less than you think!"

Second, pride nourishes a sense of superiority. When a gust of pride blows into our souls, we feel that we are somewhat better than others, that what we have surpasses what others have. Our preaching ability, the church we serve, the salary we earn, the influence we wield—each of these good things spoils under the influence of an ambition based solely on outdoing other pastors.

Third, pride thrives on the false belief that it is our own works that have given us our position, our possessions, our abilities. After the Hebrews broke free from slavery, God reminded them that they still faced the greatest risks: "Do not say to yourself, 'My power and the might of my own hand have gotten me this wealth' " (Deut. 8:17). No growth is entirely the pastor's to claim, without credit to the congregation and to the Spirit, whose ways are beyond knowing; no capability accrues within us without the guidance and example of pastors from the past; no promotion comes to us without the work and trust and risk of supervisors. Pride has us congratulating ourselves, rather than thanking God or acknowledging the help of others.

Fourth, pride deepens in us the egocentric view that the whole world revolves around us. All our musings and conversations and work revolve around *our* skills, *our* desires, *our* understanding of what ought to be done. Pastors smitten by pride reveal in subtle ways the underlying view that their church exists to serve them, their denomination's purpose is to provide for them, their supervisor's eye should be focused exclusively on them.

Pride elicits anger from those around it, sadness for those who understand it, and loneliness for those who practice it.

In pride's grasp, we lose the Christian sense of empathy and compassion because we are too focused on our own needs to pay attention to what goes on inside someone else. When I am consumed with myself, our mutuality is undermined, for I find joy only in *my* accomplishment and not yours, *my* work and not yours. Pride pushes away any suggestion that the work is *ours* together.

Pride corrupts our ambitions by steering us toward activities that serve ourselves. All actions are evaluated by their effect, positive or negative, on ourselves, rather than on promoting God's will. Therefore, it points us toward the wrong things—position for sake of being above others, salary for sake of making more than others. It feeds that temporary sense of euphoria that comes with outdoing, outranking, outperforming someone else. Pride would have kept Jesus away from the tax collectors, restrained him from washing his disciples' feet, and prohibited his sacrifice on the cross.

For as long as human beings have monitored the movements of the soul, they have seen pride fuel ambitions toward unhealthy goals. The Genesis promise that "you will be like God" (3:5) awakened the desires and appetites of Adam and Eve, enticing them to rebel. Obsessed with their own aspirations, the people who built the tower of Babel had said, "Let us make a name for ourselves" (Gen. 11:4), but only tumbled back into confusion and strife.

Jesus squelches aspirations to prideful place, admonishing his disciples not to sit "at the place of honor . . . for all who exalt themselves will be humbled, and those who humble themselves will be exalted" (Luke 14:8b, 11). And he warns against "practicing your piety before others in order to be seen by them" (Matt. 6:1).

When James and John decided to move closer to Jesus, it was a commendable and inspired ambition. But when they desired to sit *closest* to Jesus, their focus changed. Rather than looking to Jesus, they glanced furtively over their shoulders at the other disciples, anticipating that their own spiritual accomplishments had markedly overshadowed everyone else's. Pride redirects ambitions.

And Paul reminds his brothers and sisters:

> Do nothing from selfish ambition or conceit, but in humility regard others as better than yourselves. Let each of you look not to your own interests, but to the interests of others.
> What do you have that you did not receive? And if you received it, why do you boast as if it were not a gift?
> (Phil. 2:3-4; I Cor. 4:7b, c)

Pastors who use sermons to tell self-indulgent stories, those who take credit for that which was the work of many others, those who hype-up statistics in ways that everyone knows are not true—in these instances, we feel pushed away, shut out. Who wants to share ministry with someone who can only boast? It's hard to share our real selves, including our disappointments, with those who gloat about their successes. Pride creates a gulf between us, over which only sparks of animosity seem to arc. When James and John asked Jesus if they could sit on his right and left in his glory, a river of resentment poured forth from the other disciples.

Once when a group of pastors met for breakfast, it was mentioned that one pastor had graduated from a different seminary from the others. No one thought anything of it. But then he began to boast about his seminary. He talked with intensity, as if arguing, about the soundness of his professors. With something little short of panic, he bragged that his seminary had the best biblical-studies department and the most effective field-service program. The more savage his manner, the more decidedly uneasy the other pastors became. They looked around at one another, some baffled, others gathering their armies for counter attack. But the one pastor continued, blind to the mounting jeopardy toward which his tongue was taking him.

We can go on in the same way about our families or careers or possessions, our church statistics or preaching or administrative finesse—press all the advantages, lift high our special prowess. Some pastors are always selling themselves. The more desperate our situation, the more unrestrained our boasting. Pride covers an essential hunger, a desperate loneliness, a fear of inferiority. It is a symptom of suffering.

All of us have advantages that others do not, born of our experience, training, relationships, natural talents. How easily our pride causes us to misuse them.

Just out of seminary, I pastored a church larger than most recent graduates serve. One day some pastors were talking about a mistake some pastor had made in another parish, and I remarked, jokingly, that if I did that, I'd find myself booted to Blank Church, quick as a flash. But I used the name of a small church significantly less attractive than my own appointment, by most measures. Everyone laughed. My manner and tone had left no doubt about the superiority of my present appointment.

Afterward, an older pastor took me aside. Unknown to me, he had served Blank Church for several years during middle age. He told me that Blank Church was not really as bad as I thought. He had learned humility and patience there, he said. Blank Church had taught him many lessons I would never have the opportunity to learn, since I had started with such a large church, and it required skills I would never develop. And that was my loss.

He was right. Every word he spoke tore straight to the target. I had created a distance between us with words sent spinning in a flash of pride. More than a lack of tact, my words had revealed something deeper that the pastor had seen and had the courage to challenge—the proud assumption that what I had and what I did was somehow better or higher.

James and John must have felt the heat of shame when they

faced the other disciples after their self-serving request. Cut to the core by the sensation of being alone, their own pride had unbound the tie that had blessed them.

In a strange spiritual paradox, the pride that asserts how wonderful we are springs from a deep sense of inadequacy, a lingering doubt deep inside that what we have and do is not enough. The emptiness remains until the day we see it for what it is, and we realize that it is God's grace that saves us, and not our works; God's sacrifice in Jesus Christ gives us our only cause for boasting.

Envy

If pride is our excessive preoccupation with *our own* accomplishments, possessions, abilities, or honors, then envy describes our excessive preoccupation with *someone else's* accomplishments, possessions, abilities, or honors. Through the eyes of envy, we peer longingly at the grass that seems so much greener on the other side of the fence. What belongs to another—another pastor's church, salary, position, ability— inspires our hunger and our hatred. Envy is the writhing inside, the internal outcry, the reflexive response *inside* us provoked by something *out there*. It ties our spirit and our happiness to what happens in someone else's life, especially another's successes and acquisitions. It's not that *we need* those things, but that they *have* them, that sets our emotions and impulses swirling.

At every window, we see what we want but will never possess. Drilled by the urge to acquire or achieve what someone else has, we pursue goals that recede with every step, until we pass the recognized borders of propriety. There is always someone somewhere who has more, who does better. Insatiability is the essence of envy, and envy is a sorrow we feel. It is the opposite of charity, since charity rejoices at a neighbor's good fortune, but envy grieves over it.[1]

Stories of bloody envy pour from each page of the Bible. Between the first brothers, it led to violence. Cain could not tolerate feeling second best.

The Ten Commandments warn against stealing, but also

foretell the spiritual death which comes, not just from *taking* what belongs to another, but from *wanting* what belongs to another—"You shall not covet . . . anything that belongs to your neighbor" (Exod. 20:17). When we seek to satiate our ambitions without considering the effect on our neighbors, we bring destruction upon ourselves.

Anyone who has ever longed for something another possesses can understand the resentful and sullen Ahab, in the story of Naboth's vineyard. Sleeplessly obsessed, he finds no peace as long as he does not own what Naboth has.

Jesus acknowledges the viperous powers of envy when he speaks against the grumbling of the laborers in the vineyard who see others receive the same reward for less work. Paul writes that "love is not envious or boastful" (I Cor. 13:4).

Envy threatens our spirits in a number of ways. First, it causes continuing unhappiness with ourselves. When we look into the lives and churches of other pastors, we see a thousand reminders of things we wish we could do as well, or things we wish we had. Like Ahab, who concentrated on the one thing he lacked, unable to see that the whole kingdom was his, we are denied a sense of satisfaction in our own churches and our own talents.

Second, envy causes us to squander our resources on that which does not satisfy. We step into someone's parsonage so much more beautiful than our own, or we feel overcome by the size of another pastor's sanctuary, the strength of another pastor's preaching. Envy alters our perspective by just a few degrees, gently edging up our dissatisfactions, ever so slightly whetting our appetites for things we never before missed. Left unchecked, envy engulfs us in unhappiness and elicits gargantuan appetites. We see others as provocations, reminders of what we are not.

Third, the winds of envy drive us off course, redirecting our ambitions—not according to what God would have us do, but in the direction of what another possesses. Our desire to serve God is overcome by our desire to serve First Church—not because our gifts match its needs, but because a fury of emotions rushes through us at the thought of someone else serving it. Envy takes us toward destructive destinations, down ruts dug by our resentments.

Fourth, with envy in our hearts, we cannot celebrate the victories of our brothers and sisters. Or worse, we actually despise their success. To hear that another pastor, even a friend, has received what we desired, causes an unspeakable stress.

Sometimes, in the murkier waters of our souls, swims the unspoken thought that if we can't be as successful as other pastors, then we wish that they were as unsuccessful as we are. Hatred brews in those words. Envy destroys community.

Unrestrained, these feelings pervert to an unsettling satisfaction in the difficulties of another, like the race car driver who experiences a flash of exhilaration to see an opponent spinning out of control. To know that someone who usually succeeds is struggling can fuel in the envious a wicked delight. One pastor confessed that through thirty years of ministry, he had lived with the secret hope that his predecessors and successors would not do well, so that parishioners would fondly remember his contribution to their church as outstanding.

Finally, envy causes us to sacrifice our internal measure of worth for an external measure. We live our lives in reflexive dialogue with the doings and havings of others. Our self-worth no longer springs from internal sources, but from our sense of self in comparison with others.

A pastor renowned for his preaching spoke at one gathering of ministers. He had written best-selling books and traveled widely to lead preaching missions. After his opening sermon, preachers commented in the hallway: "I'm disappointed. That was terrible." "That wasn't so special, anybody could do that." "It's just that he has all that time to work on his sermons, since his staff does all the work."

With such comments, pastors reveal more about themselves than about a guest speaker. We avoid overrating our brothers and sisters for fear we may reveal our own lesser competencies. Out of sheer envy, we pine after others' talent and fame.

All of us have heard other pastors preach mesmerizing sermons—theologically sound, deeply relevant, carefully crafted—and sometimes with a light shining so brightly before us, our own efforts appear lackluster. Even though such preachers may have advantages of experience and education we cannot match, we set our work beside theirs, and our sermons seem lifeless, pale, empty. Envy chokes creativity. Envy makes us angry at ourselves, resentful at the person who does better, downcast about our prospects for a happier life. Envy causes us to want to be what we were never created to be—someone else.

If our burning pride and envy need more kindling, *comparison* is sure to help. It is the starting point for either sin. Post a list of people in order of rank or salary, and immediately the flames of pride and envy leap to new life. If we take satisfaction in ranking above others on the list, we open ourselves to pride. We feel superior, satisfied in our abilities. If we see that others rank above us, we open ourselves to envy, to resentment at others and dissatisfaction with ourselves.

Many practices foster comparison among pastors. One of the more insidious devices is a listing of pastors' salaries, from largest to smallest, which some supervisors distribute to pastors and laity. The morale problems that grow from this material comparison are traumatic. It makes a mockery of covenantal ministry. It leads to a sense of injustice as each pastor identifies people "above" him or her who have lesser gifts and abilities, and it fosters fear and insecurity as those "below" with greater gifts are identified. It narrows the goals of ministry and the aspirations of our calling to a single unreliable criterion of success—salaries. Pride and envy are invited in when our ambitions are refocused toward lesser ends.

Greed

Picture a nest crowded with baby birds, their eyes closed, their throats open wide. Trembling with hunger, they desperately trill for food, each seeking to push ahead of the others. Their beaks, gaping wide, seem too large for their tiny bodies. In the frenzy of feeding, each fledgling is all throat, insatiable appetite.

The Old Testament word for human being is *nephesh,* and it finds its roots in a Hebrew word that originally meant "throat, gullet." Whenever I contemplate *nephesh,* I see those tiny fuzzy balls of frenzied appetites, climbing over one another, chirping for more and more. What more appropriate description of the human situation! We are all appetite, gullets gaping wide, hungry for more, for better.

When our appetites lead us toward selfish pursuits, we fall into greed. While envy has a personal dimension (I want something you have), greed is more general (I want something, whether you or anyone else now has it).[2] Anything can be the object of our avarice—money, possessions, power, prestige, position, even relationships (where greed overspills into lust).

Greed grows from a sense that before we can find happiness, we need to obtain something we lack. Greed makes us think that things we own will fill up those hollow parts of our hearts.

The suffering of greed is such that even when appetites are temporarily satiated, the hunger remains and directs itself toward desiring even more. So we lurch back and forth, grasping, holding, then hungering again.

The tempter of Adam and Eve symbolizes unending appetite. A snake is nothing but an esophagus, serving no other purpose but to consume. The founders of our faith were saying, "We're like that inside—all appetite."

The prophets decry the selfishness that blinds us to our responsibilities toward the widow and orphan, the stranger and the poor. They knew that greed brings personal grief and calamity to community. And Jesus repeatedly warned against pursuing that which does not satisfy the human spirit:

> Do not store up for yourselves treasures on earth, where moth and rust consume . . . but store up for yourselves treasures in heaven.
>
> For what will it profit them if they gain the whole world but forfeit their life?
>
> No one can serve two masters; for a slave will either hate the one and love the other, or be devoted to the one and despise the other. You cannot serve God and wealth.
>
> (Matt. 6:19a-20; 16:26; 6:24)

Paul clarifies the risks of unbridled appetites and selfish ambitions. Of the enemies of Christ, he writes, "Their god is the belly" (Phil. 3:19b). He warns against the wrong objects of ambition: "For the love of money is a root of all kinds of evil, and in their eagerness to be rich some have wandered away from the faith and pierced themselves with many pains" (I Tim. 6:10). He offers himself as an example of satisfied living: "For I have learned to be content with whatever I have"—a poignant message from someone in prison (Phil. 4:11b).

Greed has become culturally acceptable, and we have legitimized its many forms in the church, sanctifying selfish ambitions with the language of sacrifice. In thinking, "I have decided to submit to a higher responsibility," I may disguise my appetite for power and reward. Greed refocuses our values, from giving *of* ourselves to getting *for* ourselves. The media hype about the excesses of certain televangelists allows us a convenient and distant target for charges of greed in minisry. Sometimes the difference between us and them has more to do with opportunity than motive. Those pastors who press their own advantage at every turn turn Christ's admonition to "feed my sheep" into "fleece my sheep."

Greed causes us to push too much for ourselves. I heard of one pastor who made more money than any other pastor his age in his area. Things went well in his church until he demanded a pay increase that the church leaders felt the budget could not support, despite how much they valued him. But the pastor continued to push, and the increase was granted. The lay members felt alienated, the positive relationship with the church turned sour, and other pastors wondered, "Why did he need so much money? Was it worth the cost?"

We deplore those church members who, greedy for more money, devote every ounce of energy and every minute of time to their work, neglecting their families and their community obligations. Yet in our own way, we do the same to position ourselves for promotion.

In his short story "How Much Land Does a Man Require?" Leo Tolstoy tells about Pakhom, a peasant who owns only a few small acres to farm for his family's living. Pakhom concludes that he has too little land, so he saves and borrows and buys a little more. This angers the other peasants and he loses all his friends in his greed for more land. He eventually concludes that he will have to move his family somewhere else to find enough land to make him happy. So Pakhom moves to a place where land is cheaper, but not even ten times more land makes him happy.

Then he hears rumors of even better and cheaper land somewhere else, and he eventually arrives at the place of his dreams, where he can have all the land he wants. After Pakhom pays the king, he is allowed to begin at sunrise and walk in a huge circle, and all the land he can walk around before sunset will be his.

Pakhom walks quickly and steadily until mid-morning. Then he sees a beautiful ravine that he must make his own and so goes farther before circling back. In late afternoon he sees some first-rate land by a river and includes that. Before long, it is getting late, and Pakhom must run to get back to his beginning place before sunset. His appetite for land has caused him to walk too big a circle, and he runs faster and harder, but his breathing becomes labored. Finally, just as he reaches his beginning point at sunset, he falls down dead.

How much land does a person require? Pakhom is buried in a piece of land as long as the distance between the top of his head and his heels.

We move from place to place—not always because it is best for us or for our family, but because of our appetite for more. We sacrifice our friends for more. We constantly focus on what we do not possess, unable to live contentedly with what we have. And like poor Pakhom, we burn ourselves out, overreach ourselves after the wrong things, only to find that we cannot enjoy what we have grasped. Imagine what it is like to live with Pakhom!

Our minds work overtime, hiding our vices and justifying our appetites, so that it's not easy to uncover our own greed. Like pride and envy, greed reveals our essential hunger. Greed destroys community as it pushes us into direct conflict with others, creating a violent game of empty passions.

Anger

Anger springs from our inability to grasp the fact that we cannot control reality. It is the displeasure and antagonism inside us, in reaction to something that is happening that contradicts our will. People say things we do not want them to say. Programs fail that we wanted to succeed. People disapprove of what we want them to appreciate. Budgets fall short, staff members disappoint, Sunday school teachers quit—the whole world conspires against us.

Because anger comes from our unmet desire to control everything, it feeds our ambition by making us imagine that if we had *more* power, *more* control, *more* of something, then we would find peace. Ambitions pursued or achieved in anger never bring the peace we seek.

The suffering from anger comes in many ways. There is the deep, seething anger that destroys our souls over time. We all know ministers whose anger slowly consumes them. Honors fall to the wrong people. Salaries are unfair. They are not considered for churches they deserve. Decisions are made over which they have no say. Pastors the same age serve larger churches. Year after year, things happen differently from the way they had hoped, and anger simmers below the surface. Some people are angry at things that will never be resolved.

We must battle the resentments that our own unfulfilled ambitions have cultivated. Sometimes we are frustrated with ourselves for wanting so much, angry at others for attaining it, hostile toward our supervisors for overlooking us.

Anger turned inward forms a kind of depression, the deep, dark feeling of disappointment that twists through the soul like a great slow-moving river—leaden, forceful, unremitting.

Churches value pastors who are courteous, objective, and pleasant. The high premium on pastors who keep their cool produces in many of us a hidden quality, cautious and guarded, about disagreeable issues and controversial opinions. It is difficult for us to express our frustration openly and directly in the presence of church members and other clergy. And the reservoirs of anger that accumulate can overflow on our families, or we may store them up unresolved until they distill into emotional poison.

Anger is not always sinful. The prophets railed against their society's oppression in voices strong with the steel of anger. We can't say that Jesus was not Christlike when he turned the tables on the moneychangers. He expanded our understanding of Christlikeness to include anger.

Destructive anger stems from our desire to control the world. We want things on our time schedule; we want people to respond to our perfect will. And when that does not happen—and there are a thousand reminders every day that life is not like that—anger boils in our blood. The harm takes many forms.

First, deep anger isolates us. The more insistent we are upon having our own way, the more distant we grow from others, clinging to our will and pursuing it without regard to what is best and highest. Some pastors harbor so much resentment that effective ministry is impossible. Others carry among their baggage such bitter cynicism that cooperation with other pastors is out of the question. Accumulated, unresolved anger leaves us alone and desperate, with no fundamental alliances intact.

Second, anger eats us up inside. It destroys fullness of life. The offsprings of anger are anxiety, guilt, depression, sleeplessness, chronic anticipation. Our minds work overtime to replay past encounters, and our souls relish the rehearsals of battles yet to come.

Anger strains our relationship with God. It's hard to find peace when we are full of storms inside.

Sometimes we hide behind our anger. We make a mistake and explode in anger at ourselves. When people see how hard we are on ourselves, they refrain from criticism.

Or we use anger to control others. If co-workers fear that any wrong word will set off a rage, they submit in an attempt to avoid conflict.

Sometimes we use anger as a way to avoid responsibility for our actions. We scream, pound our fist, jump up and down, and then say, "I'm sorry, I guess I just lost my temper for a moment," meaning, "Don't blame me, it's this temper of mine." When an employee disappoints us, we dance around in anger, to feel we have done something about the injustice, though the problem with the person and the system persists.

Lust and Gluttony

Lust and gluttony refer to the extravagance of our physical appetites. These two sins have us wandering beyond what is necessary, ethically appropriate, or spiritually healthy.

Lust and gluttony may seem outside our discussion of ambition. But it was ambition of a sort that made David abuse his prerogatives so terribly when he panted after Bathsheba.

People overcome by lust become what they never wished to become. They risk more dearly held relationships, unable to keep perspective or consider the implications of their actions. They hurt those who stand as the object of their desires by making them the substance of imagination rather than fully balanced people. And those driven by lust, even when they find their desires fulfilled, discover that their pursuit does not satisfy their hunger as they thought it would.

Sexual lust is one of the most visible and common reasons pastors are dismissed from the ministry. At work is the unspoken thought, "If I can't have everything I want, perhaps at least I can have this person I want. If I can't fulfill my fantasy of being powerful in the world, at least I can exercise my power over this person." The vulnerability and dependency of a parishioner in need feeds this illusion of the pastor's power to rescue and heal. To the extent that such infidelities express the pastor's need to control, to feel competent and needed, this kind of relationship is deeply related to ambition.[3]

When we submit to lust or gluttony, we isolate our actions into discrete parts without seeing their relation to the larger picture. People on diets may see something they want and rationalize, "one bite won't hurt"; then later they justify another bite with the same excuse; and later again, the same. This humorous example demonstrates the ancient Greek philosophical weakness of *acrasia*, the way we deceive ourselves by focusing on the harmless individual parts, while ignoring the larger direction in which our small actions take us. We slip into things one step at a time. Preferring immediate pleasure, we fail to see how each consecutive action, which seems so innocent, leads us in the larger, more painful direction.

That's the story of gluttony, the painful pattern of addiction. That's the story of imagination, which leads to the friendly flirting that leads to infidelity and failed marriages. That's the story of greedy self-assertion, step by step leading us toward a ministry void of integrity. We never notice the boundaries of propriety until we overstep them and look back.

In a world of shortages and hunger, our extravagant appetites and life-styles raise significant questions for the conscientious follower of Christ. As we compete for salaries in North American churches, feeling that we never have enough, we forget that even the humblest American pastors fare better than most of the world's population in material goods and physical comforts.

Lust and gluttony are physical symptoms of spiritual disease, born of the ambition to have what we want when we want it, stemming from the tendency to put temporary pleasure above lasting values.

Sloth

Sloth is the temptation to diminish our lives by avoiding the harder work. Sloth refers to the intransigence of the soul, the lethargy that weighs us down until life itself becomes a deep grey bog. Paul writes, "For I do not do the good I want" (Rom. 7:19). Everything that makes for fullness of life requires sacrifice, work, involvement, risk—at least some initiative to use ourselves and our resources to their fullest. Sloth is the resistance that holds us back, keeping us from making of our lives what God wills.

The risk of sloth is not that we lose ourselves by self-propulsion, but that we lose ourselves by inertia, the failure to engage the world with our gifts and talents. Under the influence of sloth, we deny both the gift of community and the fulfillment of individuality.

Sloth is not the temptation to do nothing, so much as the temptation to do the easier job when something harder ought to be done, or to make the tough decision that will make us look bad. Through sloth, we become untrue to ourselves and unfaithful to God. Drained of enthusiasm, lacking in spirit, the slothful feel no ambition, and therefore have no will to change or improve. Pastors numbed by sloth lose no sleep while contriving new programs and spend no time above the minimum in comforting the bereaved.

Pastors paralyzed by sloth make excuses for their lack of activity: "My people really don't want me to visit them"; "There just isn't any interest in a women's group in this church"; "Only three youths were attending the fellowship meetings, so we closed them down." We take the simplest approach theologically, unwilling to grapple with more difficult issues. We just "make do" on sermon preparation, rather than putting our best effort into the most important hour of the church week. When sloth weighs us down, our reliance upon printed prayers and published sermon outlines increases with the years, rather than diminishing with experience. And we justify fishing trips and football games as time on the job, because it affords us the opportunity to visit with members.

In the strange twists the soul can take, sloth can also describe many overactive pastors. Sloth is taking the easier way. Many pastors fill their calendars with busywork, buzzing here and there to meetings, socials, and conferences, precisely to escape the more difficult issues within. Tasks like confronting our inner motivations, growing in our prayer life, working through the tangled relationships at home, seem far more threatening than leading an invocation at another dinner meeting.

Scripture commends the ardent desire to serve more fully and to use our abilities more completely in God's service. Jesus teaches this: "My Father is glorified by this, that you bear much fruit and become my disciples"; "Blessed is that slave whom his master will find at work when he arrives" (John 15:8; Matt. 24:46).

We find Jesus' clearest statement about using ourselves in the parable of the talents, which illustrates that each of us is held accountable for the way we spend our lives (Matt. 25:14-30). The reward for those who fulfill their tasks is more responsibility.

Jesus wanted his disciples to be active, not apathetic, to take initiative, not wait passively: "Ask, and it will be given you; search, and you will find; knock, and the door will be opened for you" (Matt. 7:7). His final words in Matthew's Gospel leave no room for inactivity: "Go therefore and make disciples of all nations, baptizing them . . . and teaching them" (28:19a-20).

There was an immediacy in Jesus' message and a drivenness in his work. In religion we have tended to value "the inward search over the outward act . . . centeredness and quietude over engagement and animation and struggle."[4] Perhaps we have projected this onto Jesus and consistently have lifted up his meekness, although the most compelling stories about Jesus, and the most provocative of his parables and actions, point to an active life, seizing the initiative for God's purposes.

Paul described himself before his conversion: "I advanced in Judaism beyond many among my people of the same age, for I was far more zealous for the traditions of my ancestors" (Gal. 1:14). And his ambitious nature continued after his conversion: "I worked harder than any of them" (I Cor. 15:10). He was assertive and confident, and he kept these attributes following his conversion, but with different objects.

And he expected the same from other Christian leaders: "Outdo one another in showing honor. Do not lag in zeal, be ardent in spirit, serve the Lord" (Rom. 12:10b-11). Even those who strive for high position find encouragement: "Whoever aspires to the office of bishop desires a noble task" (I Tim. 3:1).

For Paul, the strength for his work comes from God: "I can do all things through him who strengthens me" (Phil. 4:13). And the goal was the proclamation of Christ: "Thus I make it my ambition to proclaim the good news" (Rom. 15:20).

Forbidden Fruit

Some ambition is sinful because of its object; we fall too much "in love with this present world" (II Tim. 4:10). Some ambition is sinful because of our intentions; we serve "the creature rather than the Creator" (Rom. 1:25).

Some ambition begins with genuine motivation and with an object of the highest good, but becomes sinful because we are thrown off course by the temptations we carry in our hearts. Our souls plummet toward misery, fueled by a venomous mix of envy and pride, greed and anger, lust and gluttony, entangled in endless combinations.

All the deadly sins express our need to control, our frustration that life is not another way, our desire to stand at the center of the world. They all grow from our sense of inadequacy. They position us as relentlessly driven by things outside ourselves—things we own, things possessed by others, worldly comforts and abilities, attractive people, appetizing foods. All these have us putting self-gratification before the needs of community. They have us searching frantically for salvation in the material world.

To the extent that we submit to the passions of pride, envy, greed, and the others, we cut ourselves off from becoming fully human because we cut ourselves out of the community relationships that make us persons. God remains undetectable and inapproachable until we discover God in our mutuality, a mutuality that is sabotaged as long as pride and greed, envy and anger, remain unrestrained. We deny God in our tendencies that deny our mutuality.

The early Christian thinkers remind us that every time we submit to one of these sins, the tendency is strengthened, the urge is fed, the beast grows larger until it becomes even more difficult for us to break free of its grasp.

It takes a constant readjusting of our course and a continual reminder of our destination to progress despite the crosswinds. We do not see ourselves clearly unless we take these tendencies into account. We have no accurate view of Christian community unless we acknowledge that these temptations are present. A swimmer, aware of the risks of the undertow, does not stop swimming altogether, but learns how to avoid treacherous waters and watches for those tides that carry the greatest danger.

FOR PERSONAL REFLECTION OR GROUP DISCUSSION

◇

When you experience a significant career advancement or visible success in ministry, how do your peers respond? How does a sense of accomplishment influence your effectiveness? Your ambition?

◇

As you sort through disappointments you have experienced in your own advancement, what factors do you think contributed to your unhappiness? What feelings do you hold toward the clergy placement system? Toward supervisors or other pastors? How has the experience shaped your ambitions, your career expectations, your relationships with other clergy, your sense of self-affirmation? How has the experience changed you positively or negatively?

◇

Which do you think represents the greatest spiritual hazard to the effectiveness of pastors—envy, greed, or sloth? Do you find that these impulses play a role in your sense of disappointment or dissatisfaction at times? How are pride, envy, and greed symptoms of suffering?

◇

How do the spiritual hazards of pride, envy, greed, and so on, differ between women and men? Which are the most deadly to women's personal growth and ministerial effectiveness?

◇

What helps a pastor keep envy or greed from shaping aspirations? How much does comparison with other pastors (of salaries, church membership, etc.) influence a pastor's sense of satisfaction or unhappiness in ministry?

CHAPTER FOUR

Bodies and Bucks

The Struggle for Integrity

We sometimes envy people in other careers. As compared to the ministry, their goals seem so clear, their results so tangible.

Physicians can see the antibiotic they prescribe bring healing, or watch the new mother hold the baby they delivered. Architects feel the satisfaction of watching their plans move from the region of imagination to blueprints, and finally to concrete and steel. Bankers can drive through the community and point out homes and businesses financed by their work.

We expect to see fruit from our labor. We need to feel some semblance of accomplishment and attainment.

Primary Marks of Accomplishment

Pastors, like everyone else, need to know they are getting somewhere, that they are making a difference. And yet it is often difficult to tell just how much we are accomplishing. The architect can leave the dedication ceremony of a new building, saying, "I have done my job." But what is the result that sustains in us a sense of accomplishment?

Even the best sermons are slippery. It's hard to get a handle on whether they are true and effective. Sometimes when we have crafted them with our deepest insight and hardest work, we read no reaction on the faces in the crowd and hear very little response after worship. The elusive quality of our trade denies us the complete satisfaction of seeing the full impact of our work.

When we visit members in the hospital, sometimes our bedside chatter meanders from the weather to the cuisine to the difficulty in finding parking; then we offer a brief closing prayer and leave. It is difficult to discern whether we have done anything particularly Christian or worthwhile. We cannot see the long-term impact of our work. A full sense of accomplishment eludes us.

People ask questions at Bible study, and we stutter through unsure answers. Sometimes we doubt whether our study together has addressed their deepest needs. We cannot be sure whether it is our friendship, or our sincerity, or our faithfulness, or our teaching ability, or our biblical scholarship that defines our time together as "successful."

A woman comes to us for counsel about her husband's infidelity. We listen, and comment, and encourage. At what point in our conversation can we sense that we have fulfilled our mission for this person?

Our primary goals include changed hearts, minds remolded by the spirit of Christ, people renewed by a genuine experience of grace, students burrowing to new depth of insight and understanding, members stretching toward more significant service. Genuine movements Godward sometimes take years to discern. Measurements are unsure, setbacks are frequent, and progress is incalculable by either yardstick or microscope. Success at our primary task, the attainment of spiritual goals, is not always visible, immediate, tangible.

Jesus offered the parable of the sower to encourage his disciples through the doubts they experienced about their own usefulness. As they traveled two by two, some experienced tremendous success and positive response, while others encountered rejection and failure. When they returned, some jubilant and others discouraged, Jesus assured them that he considered their faithfulness in sowing seed rather than just looking at the measurable results of their labor. The parable promises that God works through us in the fullness of time to bring immeasurable harvest, even though rocky ground and ravenous birds often destroy the results we need to see for our own sense of accomplishment.

The gospel is profound. Precisely because of this profundity, it has an elusive quality which shallow assessments and short-term measures cannot fathom. The challenge is to be able to sustain our psychological, emotional, and spiritual sense of accomplishment with evidence so difficult to see.

Secondary Marks of Accomplishment

Since we cannot quantify the long-term impact of our sermons, at least we can count the number of ears that hear them. We can console ourselves with the thought that the chances of the seed taking root increase if we cover more ground and more people hear the message.

So we begin to rest our sense of accomplishment on attendance figures and membership statistics. Gospel truth may seem elusive in its effects, but in numbers, we have something tangible, measurable, almost scientifically verifiable. Numbers allow us to gauge, graph, and compute. Success becomes empirical.

The secondary symbols of achievement include the statistics on our pastoral reports, the number of people at worship and Sunday school, the level of giving, the number of people on the church staff.

These measurable signs include the building projects and facility improvements that give physical expression to our achievement. Some projects begin with the pastor's need to see progress, rather than the church's need for new space. When this "edifice complex" goes unrestrained, pastors pursue building projects, not because everything is going well, but because they suspect things are going poorly, and they need some physical reminder of their contribution. With primary symbols of achievement so elusive, at least we can look at the new education wing, smell the fresh paint, and run our fingers along the new finish on the hardwood door. For a brief moment of exultation, we can see spiritual goals poured in concrete and dabbed in paint, and we can nudge with our elbow the doctor with his babies and the architect with her blueprints and say, "That never would have happened without me." Panic recedes and we feel useful again.

Our personal trust in the secondary marks of accomplishment finds support from our denominations' dependence upon them to measure and evaluate effectiveness. Pulpit committees and supervisors depend upon numbers and concrete attainments for the same reasons we do—they are easier to measure, more objective, less elusive than the primary marks of accomplishment.

Consider the way we introduce effective pastors: "Her church has doubled its attendance in the past five years"; "He is responsible for raising $8,000 for the children's home." These evidences of success dominate our church brochures, our seminary alumni newsletters, our denominational magazines, our leadership literature, and, most important, our selection process, through which pastors are chosen to serve churches. It's a seller's market for pastors with a record of growth; those who fail to show increases are told they may no longer have what it takes to make the grade.

Usually the secondary marks of accomplishment do reflect faithfulness to the primary tasks of ministry. Increases in attendance and the congregation's enthusiasm for construction often do reflect a renewed spirit among the members and demonstrate excellent and faithful pastoral leadership.

And these secondary symbols *are* easier to show to others. We can't describe the content of all our hospital visits and hold them up to the scrutiny of objective evaluation. But we can report that our staff made 248 hospital calls last year, and that represents an 18 percent increase over the year before!

These measures for ministerial effectiveness run through our blood. We have learned to trust them, and seldom do we question them. They keep our goals easy to distinguish and our mission clear. We need not strain our eyes in a search for the ultimate, for questions of end and purpose, because they are focused instead on the step before us, a more manageable, comfortable, and immediate consideration.

But while the secondary symbols of accomplishment often reflect success in the primary mission of the church, they do so *unreliably.* Growth or decline in numbers sometimes results from circumstances far beyond the control of the pastor. We cannot calculate and control everything in the spiritual realm. Some pastors work in growing and dynamic communities which require a minimum of pastoral skill for church growth. Others labor in areas of recession, where the most gifted pastor "succeeds" if the speed at which the church is declining can be arrested.

In the current climate of church growth, sometimes church authorities do not take into account these differences in circumstances.

Once a group of pastors met with their bishop to inquire about how their work would be evaluated and what criteria would be used to make pastoral appointments. With the gravity of a general, the bishop answered that the easiest way to describe the criteria is "bodies and bucks." He said he looks at how many bodies are present in attendance and how many new ones have been added to the membership. Then he evaluates the financial circumstance of the pastor's current appointment—whether denominational obligations are paid and what level of salary the pastor receives.

Single-minded adherence to the secondary symbols of achievement invites brutal competition among pastors. It encourages pastors to skew their statistics to their advantage. It makes them too quick to add names to the membership list and too slow to remove inactives, thereby diluting the meaning of discipleship. Some pastors who fulfill the primary tasks of ministry with excellence and faithfulness are overlooked because the circumstances of their congregations militate against successful secondary accomplishments. Some pastors with an immature understanding of ministry and an unfocused ecclesiology are promoted because they use short-term growth tactics with little attention to long-term church life. Some career-minded pastors refuse churches they perceive as unable to provide the opportunity for growth that would support their image as church-growth pastors.

In undergraduate philosophy, many of us read Plato's allegory of the cave. We are slaves chained to our seats in a cave. In front of us is a blank wall, upon which shadows are projected by the fire behind us. We live cognizant only of the shadows and consider them truth, without realizing that they are imperfect and secondary reflections of reality. One day we break loose; we turn around and see the origin, the true light from which the shadows come, and we realize that the shadows we trusted have limited our understanding rather than enlightened it.

The secondary symbols of achievement are the shadows on the wall, mere reflections of our mission. The shadows are helpful—sometimes they are all we can see—but we simply cannot trust them. They only partially reflect the truth of our message, and they imperfectly measure our faithfulness in proclaiming it.

The struggle for integrity in ministry takes place at several levels. If our sense of self-esteem rests on the attainment of the primary accomplishments, and our ambitions direct us accordingly, we may never see enough tangible signs of progress to keep our spirits strong. On the other hand, the secondary marks of accomplishment offer only partial and unreliable evidence of success.

And in relation to those in authority over us, the struggle for integrity takes on new dimensions. We know how easy it is to evaluate the secondary and how difficult to judge the primary, especially from the distance of a supervisory perspective. Those in authority must defend their evaluations and recommendations with objective evidence provided only by the secondary marks. We either resent their appetite for "bodies and bucks" or we work overtime to satiate their hunger, all the while troubled by the unreliability of such measures of success.

We are called by God to fulfill the primary tasks of ministry; we are evaluated by the secondary. We struggle with which of these provides our self-validation and sense of contribution.

And finally, when we venerate the secondary marks without considering their unreliability, we feed the struggle between pastors in a way that blinds us to the gifts and tasks of community. The secondary symbols of accomplishment are quantifiable, and therefore comparable. It's a short leap from comparative to competitive.

When a competitive spirit dominates our hearts, a single number by itself seems meaningless. For a pastor to say, "I had 134 people in worship last Sunday," seems incomplete without a further statement which compares that number to the number in attendance the year before, or at another church. If 134 is more than another number, it is *good;* if it is less, it is *bad.* By itself, it means little.

Jesus said, "Where two or three are gathered," but under the influence of our comparative minds, that statement has been twisted to "where two or three *more* are gathered." We behave as if God's Spirit is present only in groups that grow numerically. Some pastors close Bible studies because only five people attend. Our ambition for numbers undermines many of our primary tasks.

Tertiary Marks of Accomplishment

Beyond the elusive primary fruit of ministry and the unreliable secondary symbols of accomplishment, we find the least dependable of all—the tertiary marks of accomplishment. These are the rewards we garner when we excel in the secondary achievements. Doing well with the secondary measures often brings increased salary, awards for church growth, recognition before our brothers and sisters, titles to be attached to our names.

If salary becomes the focus of our ambitions and our principal symbol of accomplishment in ministry, we've spun completely off the road. The size of our paycheck cannot sustain a sense of ministry. We are many steps removed from our call when tertiary awards of any type fuel our ambitions.

As Americans, it's in our bones to believe that one of the most compelling goals of our work is to increase our salaries. The fact that some pastors receive two and three times what their brothers and sisters in the ministry earn does not make us uncomfortable; it seems the natural course for careers to take: Those with more experience or more responsibility make more money. We proportion the pay for the performer to the receipts at the gate.

Sometimes our faithfulness and work result in greater

attendance, but not always; the relationship is unreliable. And sometimes when our work does result in greater attendance, our salary increases and we may receive awards and recognition, but not always. There simply is no direct path from faithfulness to worldly success. Jesus Christ makes that crystal clear.

Stephen Covey shows the paucity of the motivational tactics we've borrowed from the corporate world. He tells of a company president who complained about the lack of cooperation among his people: "They're selfish. They're defensive and resistant to authority. There's no trust."

Covey tried to understand why the level of cooperation was so low. Then he noticed a chart in the president's office. On the chart, race horses were lined up on a track, and superimposed on each horse was the face of one of the company managers. At the finish line was a beautiful travel poster of Bermuda.

At weekly meetings, the president had been telling his people, "Let's all work together." Then he would point out the chart and ask, "Now which of you is going to win the trip to Bermuda?" He wanted cooperation, but he was setting them up for competition. One manager's success meant failure for all the others.[1]

When we highlight the tertiary goals of ministry—the awards and high salaries—we do the same in our denominations. We try to harvest the fruit of cooperation from a tree that we trim and feed for competition.

Some have suggested that one way out of our churches' malaise is to revive quarterly reporting, so everyone can see which pastors' churches grow and which decline. Others have suggested that we offer rewards to pastors whose churches have the fastest growth. If these methods further narrow the goals of ministry to the secondary and tertiary accomplishments, then we sabotage our own mission. Who will rise to the top of such a system? Some few honest, hard-working pastors with excellent responses in their congregation, but also many Mathematical Magicians, Credit Grabbers, and Self-seekers.

The mystery of ministry runs deeper than the numbers and is more complicated than the tertiary goals reveal. Christ simply did not demonstrate a mission reducible to numbers or encourage a ministry that finds its validation in income and awards.

Church-Growth Pressures

The current tide of church growth has brought to shore some delicate issues related to ambition. With the numbers receding so painfully in Protestant churches over the past thirty-five years, resurgence in any form enlivens an unquestioned hope.

Church-growth consultants have provided excellent new insights and innovative methods for renewing churches, and these tactics have attracted many of our most ambitious pastors. With such a powerful new influence shaping our ambitions, our objectives, and our theology, consider the possible risks and dangers. Too frequently, sound church-growth strategies are being abused in a way that brings the secondary and tertiary marks of ministry to the foreground, at the risk of the primary marks.

A church-growth atmosphere creates new stresses on pastors by fostering among supervisors and laity a desire for tangible results, and this new emphasis has caught many pastors unprepared. The high value placed on pastors who have a record of membership increase and budgetary growth has caused others to feel they are unmarketable, inadequate, and undervalued. Sometimes the new stress is constructive and leads to the acquisition of valuable new skills; at other times, it leads to severe career and morale crises among our pastors. In either case, it shapes our ambitions.

By the Numbers

Many church-growth strategies use statistical data about the church and demographic information about the community to great effect. They pinpoint patterns of growth and highlight opportunities for evangelism. Just as a heart monitor helps a doctor understand the condition of a patient, these tools give vital information about the health of our churches.

Unfortunately, we sometimes depend too heavily upon these numbers, asking more of them than they can adequately deliver. Questions about the health of a church, about merging churches, starting churches, or closing churches are not reducible to statistical data. Some healthy churches show unfavorable numbers, and some neighborhoods that show little population growth or financial strength need ministries. State of the art marketing techniques may not take into consideration many subtleties of morale, leadership, spirit, and commitment to mission.

Using charts and formulas, church-growth experts compute strategies for growth according to the numbers. Success involves moving from static or declining numbers to increasing numbers, in any of several indexes—attendance, contributions, parking spaces, number of young adults, size of staff, and so on.

The key writers of the church-growth movement (Schaller, Wagner, McGavran) keep the primary tasks of ministry sharply in view. However, many pastors, denominational staffs, and judicatory leaders misuse statistics by considering them the only measure of church health and pastoral effectiveness. They rely upon numbers because of their expediency in facilitating evaluation and because of the influence of corporate and cultural models of success which narrow the definition of growth to expansion and increase.

Too narrow a view of success can limit our engagement in ministry. A strict results-orientation develops an affection for ministries that are measurable by numbers—new member recruitment, increased attendance—to the neglect of ministries for which the results are not so easy to determine—pastoral care, social services, teaching, care for the aged.

Such an emphasis on numbers may focus the ambitions of some pastors toward short-term gains; the statistics look good during their tenure, sometimes at the cost of long-term benefits. Powerful self-seeking ambitions may even be rewarded as evangelical impulses. Many pastors receive recognition for vast building projects which incur heavy debt, only to leave an unmanageable burden for their successors. If growth is predicated on a pastor's need to impress supervisors, attract the attention of pulpit search committees, win the approbation of the laity, or build up self-esteem, then the primary accomplishments have fallen from view, and the pastor may lead the church to programs that avoid the tougher issues.

Statistics alone fail to take into consideration the nature of the ministry that is offered. When a church's primary reputation in a community grows from its excellent handball courts, great gym, and good aerobics training, its strong numbers may disguise a weak witness. When attendance in youth groups is sustained by a succession of ski trips and travels to Disney World, the numbers-orientation applauds what may be a program empty of substance. Sometimes a ministry reducible to numbers causes churches to avoid controversial issues. More writers than John C. Harris may believe that "there must be a shift that accords the aggressive development of the quality of congregational life a status equal to the production of growth and income."[2]

The myth that growth in churches takes place only when more members join focuses our ambitions too narrowly. A healthy church may grow in its compassion and its capacity to care for AIDS victims, or it may experience a deepening in faith, or a growth in its passion for the stewardship of God's natural world. It is likely that such a church might see a corresponding growth in participation. Its numerical increase then would be a result of its faithfulness, not its single-minded goal.

I heard of one pastor who actually described his secret for successful evangelism. When he hired an associate pastor, he told her, "I expect to see four new members join the church each Sunday morning. If after six months we have not reached that average, you will need to look for another position."

Jesus did not coerce his disciples into evangelistic fervor by threats. Whose ambitions are we feeding? Numbers can serve us, but they cannot lead us. They can offer a partial measure of progress, but they cannot adequately define success or shape our ambitions.

Leadership

Many supervisors describe the ideal pastor to serve a growing church with characteristics that deserve careful reflection.

"We need more entrepreneurial pastors." The word *entrepreneurial* tilts toward the individualistic, a person propelled by ambitions independent of others. An entrepreneurial football star is not a team player, but one who manipulates for the most favorable contracts and lucrative commercial sponsorships. The entrepreneurial model lifts high the authority of the independent individual over covenantal ministry.

The last thing that high-strung, workaholic, career-driven suburbanites need is a high-strung, workaholic, career-driven pastor. Families suffocating under the anxieties brought on by their materialistic drive for success do not need their compulsive behaviors applauded by spiritual leaders.

If, by *entrepreneurial*, we mean pastors who are passionate and creative, those with a zealous enthusiasm for proclaiming the gospel, then let us support and encourage such models for evangelism. But self-serving and destructively compulsive behaviors in the ministry need to be restrained, or even condemned. Entrepreneurial pastors who view their ministry as sole proprietors view a franchise, sharpening their skills to outsell their competitors, undermine our mission.

"We need pastors with vision." This is true, without question. With too narrow an ambition, the vision that we call for may mean only that the pastor sees a huge church where a small one now sits.

Recently the *Wall Street Journal* reported on a megachurch in a large city which arose when a pastor of vision pressed for $32 million to fund a health club, gymnasiums, and expansive parking. He sent parking teams to Disney World to learn how to guide large numbers of cars through the weekly maze. The tone of the article is extremely cynical toward the motives and ambitions of the pastor.

Vision may include a sense of a church's possibilities for growth. It may also include the picture of a predominantly white congregation in a predominantly Hispanic community, finally coming to terms with its subtle exclusionary practices. This vision may not lead to instant increases in attendance, but it may be more true to the spirit of Pentecost. Pastoral vision cannot be narrowed to size and numbers.

Market-driven Ministry

By caressing people's tastes in recreation, music, entertainment, and life-style, the church determines the programs that will attract a particular target population. Market surveys show that young adults are acutely health conscious. Therefore the church offers basketball teams, soccer for the kids, yoga, even karate classes. Surveys show that baby boomers like a quicker pace, so we eliminate silent prayer from our worship. As if we can grip people by the sheer quantity of trifle, we carefully consider staging, color, movement, sound, costume, lighting, and greenery, to create a worship mood that replicates theater and concert.

Recently one pastor contemplated giving up communion at the principal morning service because attendance on communion Sundays lags behind the other Sundays of the month. Liturgy in pure pursuit of numbers is seldom faithful.

It is indeed prudent to consider the effect of our actions on attendance, but we neglect many primary tasks of ministry when we consider attendance the most important criterion in every instance. Increased attendance is not the right remedy to every possible congregational ill. We focus our ambitions too narrowly.

Perhaps our most profound purpose as pastors is to attract and involve more people in the life of the church and in the life of Christ, bring more people to a deeper awareness of the gifts and tasks of God's grace. The risk we face is that our desire to be successful, appealing, liked, dependable, and popular may cause us to avoid courageous action, to neglect profound personal-growth and social-justice issues, simply in order to reflect popular sentiment (what people find appealing) and attain productive measure (increased numbers). If the capacity to risk exceptional (and perhaps unpopular) action lies dormant, the pastor's power to lead a congregation toward significant ministry diminishes. Pastors lose their inner strength and passion, and churches lose the benefit of exceptional leadership when our ministries do not ultimately help people grapple with significant personal and social issues.

Theological Underpinnings

Our actions reveal an ecclesiology, an explicit or implicit understanding of the nature of the church. We need to examine whether it is true that every growing church is faithful and every faithful church is growing numerically.

If we are not careful, our churches fall into corporate selfishness, a gathering of individually generous people who, nevertheless, work together in a selfish manner. When the men's group raises money to paint the youth room, and the youth group works to help the women's group clean the kitchen, and a Sunday school class raises money for a church oven, each act represents the generous contribution of individuals who give their time and money unselfishly.

But when all that time and money circulates within the walls of the church, the result of the individual generosities is corporate selfishness. The same is true when churches spend lavish amounts on racketball courts, running tracks, renovation, and parking lots. We stretch the truth too far to justify all this as mission. Whose ambitions are we striving to fulfill?

Our actions communicate a subtle soteriology. Suppose someone responds to an advertisement, joins a yoga class, responds positively to the visitation team, eventually attends a Sunday school class for singles, attends dinners, takes trips, joins the church, and finally volunteers to help bring new people into the church. In this pattern, it is important to reflect on what salvation means and where it appears in the process. At what point has the church "succeeded" with this person? What is the goal toward which we move? Is the goal a distinct change in the person, or is it the number of persons that can be counted as they move through the system?

Perhaps there is such a thing as selfish evangelism, the desire for new members so that *we* grow rather than decline, so that *our* enthusiasm is fanned to greater fervor, or so that our career ambitions are fulfilled.

Our Witness

We should not avoid church-growth strategies. They offer pastors valuable tools that are needed as we approach a new century. And they inspire in us an appetite for evangelism and a renewed passion for outreach. These methods serve us well when used properly. But we must use them reflectively, considering why we do what we do. Our ministry springs from the primary accomplishments. If we redirect our energies toward the secondary measurements, or worse, the tertiary awards, then we build a church that is hollow and weak.

This risk is more real than we often realize. Many growing churches arise from a blitz of advertising, unsubstantiated by ministry and commitment. We've all known pastors who arrive on the scene in a flurry of activity, with skyrocketing statistics. After short pastorates, they leave, and upon their departure, the bubble bursts. We have gained nothing if attendance falls by 100 in the church they leave so that attendance may grow by 100 in a church somewhere else.

I am not writing as someone who cannot or does not practice church-growth techniques. I have no intention of confirming the intransigence of spirit that keeps some pastors from working toward faithful evangelism. Cynicism and sloth too often converge in simple rationalizations, such as "God is just interested in faithfulness, not results." These need not be exclusive choices.

I only ask us to consider what ambitions feed our *obsession* for church growth. Do we picture the individual soul, cut off from God, removed from community, barren of the Spirit's vital breath? Or are we motivated by fear of the church's death, or our own need to succeed, or society's view of progress? Is it personal gain we pursue? What ambitions are we seeking to fulfill with our church-growth orientation?

We should expect the church to grow. We should pray for growth, work for it, strive for it, and sacrifice for it. But we cannot let society's measures alone define *growth*. The meaning of growth in the church cannot be compressed to numerical measures. Increased pastoral faithfulness and effectiveness cannot be motivated solely by salary, promotion, and recognition.

The primary marks of ministry are those for which we have been called, chosen, sent. All our pledges at ordination speak of the primary marks. All the spiritual admonitions to the first disciples focused on the primary marks. We cannot depend upon the secondary and tertiary for long without the primary. Unless our work is embedded in a profound theology and rooted in our commitment to serve Christ, we plant our seeds in shallow soil.

We risk becoming a one dimensional church when we use the standards of success borrowed from the corporate world, see numerical growth as the only criterion for placing pastors, and bargain for star preachers like players in the football draft. This destroys our greatest witness.

Our contribution is not our efficiency—we have borrowed what we know of that from the corporate world. Our witness is not our marketing strategy—this we are still learning from the product managers. Our gift to the world is not our structure—every church hierarchy is a copy of a political, military, or corporate model.

Our unique contribution is our understanding of the person, in relation to God and to others, as we have experienced this in the life, death, and resurrection of Jesus Christ. We dare do nothing that sways us from this essential witness.

FOR PERSONAL REFLECTION AND GROUP DISCUSSION

◇

What does it mean to succeed in ministry? How do church members measure their pastor's success? How do supervisors evaluate success? What experiences or results make you feel that you have succeeded in ministry? From what do we derive our definitions of success in ministry? How are these definitions changing?

◇

To what extent do you think salary effects performance in ministry? What do you see as the connection between salary and clergy morale? How do our salary systems enhance or diminish mutuality in the covenant of pastors? What accounts for the preoccupation with salary that so many pastors have? What is the place of awards and recognition in the formation of more effective pastors?

◇

What causes a pastor to shift focus from the primary marks of accomplishment to the tertiary? What might cause a pastor to shift ambitions from the tertiary to the primary? What satisfactions do you find in the primary marks of accomplishment? In the secondary? The tertiary?

◇

How do you evaluate the results of evangelism efforts in your own ministry? What motivates your personal witness when you describe your faith or proclaim the gospel to others? Has ambition ever blocked or enhanced your efforts?

CHAPTER FIVE

Influence Peddlers and Mathematical Magicians

The Politics of Ministry

D enominational politics ranks high among the things pastors love to hate. We may find satisfaction in preaching, teaching, and pastoral care, but mention the conduct of business or the placement of pastors at the conference, presbytery, district, or diocese level, and pastors inevitably display a common disgust for the maneuvering and strategizing that characterize the politics of ministry.

We reveal a crippling ambivalence about this portion of our community life. We hate it, and yet we expend tremendous energy talking about it among ourselves. We deride politicking and yet we all practice it to some degree.

When asked to describe political pastors, most ministers draw an unattractive picture. We speak of craftiness in disproportionately influencing outcomes. Political pastors are sagacious, shrewd, able to see implications in actions that are not obvious to others. They are attuned to the subtleties of our interactions and operate below the surface of conversations, behind the scenes at debates. Political pastors are often seen as insincere and self-seeking. Much of the darkness of these descriptions derives from the hidden quality of political maneuvering.

On further reflection, most of us go on to recall pastors who use their political skills for positive purposes. They use power to persuade and influence people toward important ends.

They keep abreast of the issues. They take initiative, they build consensus, they know the structures of organizations. And beyond technical proficiency, they depend upon their intuitive insight. Astute pastors know the nuances of organizational life and the spirit of the people well enough to navigate successfully toward objectives.

Through politics, we shape the policies and actions of an organization; we form consensus and establish plans and carry them through. Politics is inescapably part of working in groups, and therefore it is part of our work as pastors.

Power

Power is the capacity to influence people to attain objectives. Sometimes we influence one another explicitly, and at other times more subtly; sometimes coercively, and at other times, we elicit responses by appealing to values—sometimes toward good ends and sometimes toward bad. Power is not a possession one person has and another does not. It is impossible to live outside of power relationships, and thus we cannot live without exercising power in some degree.[1]

Women's issues have made us more aware of the way power shapes everyday relationships. In a marriage, the one who handles the checkbook or drives the car or holds the TV remote control—all these things reveal explicit or implicit power relationships between women and men.

Sometimes power is a result of the position of authority we hold or our particular skill or special knowledge. Sometimes power comes from our personality or our integrity or our ability to articulate. Age, race, and sex grant certain kinds of power while limiting others.

We often think of power as an essentially untamed and brutish aspect of human relationships which has no place in church life. We find our possession and exercise of power difficult to admit and awkward to handle. But when we deny the presence of power in the church or fail to recognize it, we also deny the corrections of theological criticism and the spiritual disciplines by which we are able to channel power in constructive ways for the edification of our common life.[2]

Power becomes a tool by which many can fulfill their ambitions, and church politics provides the arena for this. Power and politics draw out the ambitious.

To pastors, denominational politics sometimes seems more intriguing than local church politics, especially if the denominational hierarchy is the arena for decisions about placement and advancement. Pastors must become aware of the institutional pressures that shape their ambitions, either by shutting down their capacity for courage and independence or by narrowing their ambitious impulses to the types of work valued by their superiors.

Politics and power—each of these terms enjoys an essential neutrality. Like ambition, either may be used for pursuing the highest of goals, or the lowest. Power can be used well or misused terribly; politics can be manipulative and dishonest or upbuilding and value-based; ambition can be greedy or self-sacrificing. In each case, it is the intention, the ends, and the means that raise ethical questions, not the mere presence of power, politics, or ambition. Mother Teresa, Mahatma Gandhi, and Martin Luther King, Jr.—all exercised immeasurable power and were well-practiced in politics.

Consider the following examples of pastors at work. Would we call these practices political? Consider the use of power. Reflect on the ambitions of the actors. How might we evaluate the appropriateness of their actions?

Prudent Self-assertiveness

Linda, a seminarian soon to graduate, writes an unsolicited letter to those responsible for ministerial placement in her denomination. She introduces herself and includes a resume of her educational and work experience. She particularly wants a position as associate pastor with Christian education responsibilities, so she spells this out clearly.

Those responsible for ministerial placement meet on the seminary campus. Linda introduces herself to as many of these people as possible so that they will know her when her name is discussed for a church.

Linda graduates and receives a position as associate pastor, as she had hoped. In her second year, she attends a gathering of pastors and hears the area supervisor propose a workshop to teach ministers about Christian education curriculum. Since this is her special interest, she approaches her supervisor after the meeting and offers to lead the workshop.

As part of her interest in educational ministries, Linda develops a plan to launch neighborhood Bible schools in some of the poorer areas of the city. Area pastors have little enthusiasm for this ministry, so Linda visits each one to explain the program and solicit support for the project.

After four years as associate pastor, Linda hears that a pastor will soon retire from a nearby church. She knows the church and its potential, and feels that the time is right in her own ministry for such a change. She meets with her supervisor on her own initiative and describes her interest in the other church, explaining her experience and outlining some of the gifts she feels she has to offer.

The initial letter, the mingling with denominational officials, the volunteering to help with a workshop, the solicitation of support for her mission project, the offer to serve another church—all Linda's actions have political implications. At each step, she has asserted her power. Her ambitions seem moderate.

Most pastors see Linda's actions as appropriate and expected. They are expressive of her faith and consistent with her abilities. They are not destructive to her relations with other pastors. One could argue that for Linda to fail to do some of these things would show an inappropriate restraint and would cheat the church of her gifts.

The Politics of Servanthood

Consider Mark, a pastor deeply moved by the plight of Haitian refugees, an issue extremely unpopular among most lay people and many pastors. Mark gives his time to help refugees find food and shelter. He mentions the needs of refugees to the church members during Bible studies. He involves members in the desperate needs of these people, soliciting blankets, organizing food drives.

Soon older women are knitting baby clothes for refugee children and young men are loading food supplies. Mark has built a consensus of conscience.

Next he works with denominational relief committees. He visits individual pastors to elicit their involvement, and despite resistance at every turn, he progresses toward a wider ministry. He receives no acclaim for his work—no new titles, no additional salary—but enjoys a quiet sense of self-affirmation, a deep sense of fulfilling God's call.

Mark's step by step progression reveals strategic political planning and a careful use of power to address real-life needs in a controversial situation. Would we think of Mark as ambitious?

Mark distinguishes his *interests* from his *self-interests*. He considers serving refugees to be in his interests, and so he speaks for them, supports them, defends them. These are not selfish goals. Our *interests* come from the values we hold.

Some argue that it is in the interests of the United States to support human rights and to influence all countries, both allies and adversaries, to stop abuses. Human rights are in our national *interests* because they are part of our Constitution, expressive of our deepest commitments.

Others argue that insisting on human rights is not in our national *self-interests*, because it jeopardizes our nation's relationship with governments we need to work with toward other objectives.

Sometimes our *interests* and our *self-interests* are the same. At other times they are in conflict. Because of Mark's involvement in unpopular issues, many churches are less than enthusiastic to have him as their pastor, but this does not deter him in his work.

Pursuing only *self-interests* is the most common corruption of power, politics, and ambition.

The Corruption of Politics

The examples above demonstrate that every pastor, including the most genuine and faithful, participates in politics, exercises power, and expresses ambition. If this is the case, why do we have such a strong distaste for the political side of our work?

Anger about ministerial politics is not directed at pastors like Linda and Mark, but grows from the fact that some of the most visible practitioners of the politics of ministry do not work out of faithful commitment to anything but themselves.

Consider each of these political pastors and whether you have ever met them.

The Self-seeker

Self-seekers measure every activity according to its impact on their careers. Their preoccupation with promotion is more important than any achievement in the tasks of ministry. "How should I vote on this issue? What should I say in this debate? Should I chair this committee? Where should I sit at the luncheon? Do I need to be seen at this pastor's funeral?" Self-seekers evaluate every action—not according to ethics or faith or friendship, but according to the benefit for themselves that may accrue from their decision.

Self-seekers offer themselves generously to help with projects and committees that are popular and visible, but avoid those that are mundane or controversial. If the salary is right and the risks are low, they place their names into consideration for every major church, without assessing their gifts or the needs of the church.

Self-seekers even measure the value of relationships according to this formula. At clergy assemblies, they interrupt their conversations with pastors of "lower rank" for any opportunity to patronize those they perceive to have greater influence. They are ambitious for their own promotion.

The Influence Peddler

Sometimes it takes a while to discern the Influence Peddlers in a gathering of pastors. They seldom speak before a group themselves, preferring to send their soldiers to the front. They influence outcomes while avoiding the attendant risks of losing face. Since their intentions are not clear enough to challenge, they avoid direct vulnerability.

Influence Peddlers trade us their support for our projects if we promise our support for theirs. This reasonable-sounding political move can tie together two unrelated measures in artificial and sometimes destructive ways. If we promise to support them in the future while they support us now, we may find ourselves voting for things we otherwise never would support. When we vote to pay our dues, we've been manipulated.

The word *manipulate* comes from the Latin word for hand. Manipulators move others through their fingers like chess pieces. Manipulative pastors use other people—pastors, laity, and supervisors—for their own ambitions.

The Wily Politico

Wily Politicos thrive on the underside of ministry. Competition between pastors makes their blood run hot. They pant after political gossip, always carrying with them a bag of current stories about who wants to move where, which pastors are striving for what. They know by heart all the salaries and all the perks of all the churches. They exegete the patterns of power, knowing who makes the decisions and what their inclinations may be.

They stand ready to advise others about what they should consider as they contemplate pastorates. Their insider information astonishes everyone. Wily Politicos trade information like baseball cards, depending on constant communication with others like themselves. To them, everything has political implications.

Who will go where is a Wily Politico's constant concern. Such pastors sprinkle their conversations with references to gifts, talents, and ministry, to camouflage their intentions. We never know how our words will be taken by them; we only know that what we say will be computed through a plethora of permutations for possible moves. Like bookies taking bets, they busily gather and pass out information to fuel the appetites and fears of pastors. They enjoy lighting the fires of other people's ambitions, while they stand back to watch the blaze.

The Mathematical Magician

Mathematical Magicians can manipulate virtually any set of statistics until they come out positive for themselves. One pastor reported that his church's rate of new members so far this year had increased by 50 percent, and the youth program had grown over 30 percent. Everyone was dazzled as the fountain of numbers continued to spill forth with the details he adored, calculated with a precision any market analyst would envy. His colleagues were amazed at this positive outcome, when so many had perceived the church as struggling.

Afterward, someone asked the pastor about the considerable growth. He explained that last year, two people had joined during January and February, but this year, three people joined—thus a 50 percent increase. And two youths had moved from sixth grade into seventh, joining the six already in the group, to increase it by 33 percent!

Mathematical Magicians squeeze growth out of the scantiest responses to their programs. They offer statistics on everything to continually confirm progress before their peers. The intention to mislead, to leave a wrong impression, is unethical. What does it say about pastors, our ambitions, and our definition of success, when we reformulate statistics in such a way? What does it say about our church, when pastors feel pressured by their supervisors to make things appear more positive than they actually are?

The Rumor Monger

Rumor Mongers thrive on the tribulations of their brothers and sisters in ministry. They feel few compunctions about revealing even the most intimate details of other pastors' affairs and infidelities. They enjoy rumors, half-truths, and scuttlebutt. That something is interesting matters more than whether it is true.

They sift through conversations, hoping to find a word about marital distress, tension between a pastor and congregation, competition between pastors, rumors that someone needs to move because of health. Their talk has a tabloid-like quality. Rumor Mongers are notoriously loose with confidences; for them, a secret is something to tell only one person at a time. To share our successes with such pastors is throwing pearls before swine. To reveal our failures is handing out ammunition for our own assassination.

The Credit Grabber

Credit Grabbers want their names on everything good. They thrive on positive recognition. Under their churches in the yellow pages, the first information listed is the pastor's name. They enjoy titles, and continue to wear them, whether in or out of fashion.

Credit Grabbers ride the waves as they crest. They move from issue to issue, according to what the laity applauds or their supervisors support. They run to carry the flag after the hill has already been taken.

When they arrive at a church, Credit Grabbers denigrate their predecessors, describing what bad shape the finances were in, how glad everyone was for the change, how carelessly the records were kept. Everything positive in the church's life begins, of course, the day the Credit Grabber arrives. Their highest ambition is to be well-known.

The Spiteful Malcontent

Every political arena has silent saboteurs who contribute little but criticize virtually everything put forward by others. These Spiteful Malcontents feel burned by the system, unfairly treated, and they respond with a cynicism that puts everyone else down at every opportunity. Their unstated ambition is to undermine those they resent.

Sometimes they store up these seething emotions for years until they boil over with bristling anger. They feel so frustrated when less deserving pastors get promotions that they can hardly concentrate on their work. They moan when younger pastors advance beyond them. Their own unfulfilled ambitions, like untreated ulcers, eat away through the years until it is too late to change careers and too soon to retire. With abilities unimpaired but commitments lagging, they drag across the finish line, burnt up by the race.

The Maliciously Compliant

Close relations of Spiteful Malcontents, the Maliciously Compliant are distinguished by their overt assent to expectations and demands, an assent which shields their inner disagreement and disgust. On the surface, they support their superiors and go along with the majority, while underneath they are seething with rebellious and angry impulses. They are unable to express their personal needs or articulate their point of view, and because they lack the personal autonomy and strength to disagree openly, they are compelled to submit while feeling resentful and depressed. Their ambitions are blunted by suppressing their own inner impulses and devaluing their own judgments.

The Favor Currier

Favor Curriers come in two subspecies. The more aggressive and intentional Favor Curriers "press the flesh" at every gathering of pastors, shaking hands like a politician stumping for votes. The artificial nature of their perfunctory handshakes and solicitous embraces seldom deceives their sisters and brothers in ministry.

But currying favor can take a more subtle form. Some pastors, dominated by fear of criticism or conflict, curry favor to avoid any unpleasantness or tension. They remain noncommittal on important issues because they do not want to alienate anyone. They leave the floor of meetings during votes on controversial issues so that no one sees how they stand. Trying to win friends by avoiding disagreement, they unintentionally create distance and mistrust.

Fear shuts down their own personal power and deadens their capacity for influence. Fear blurs their ability to distinguish between what is best for the church and what influential pastors, superiors, or lay people want. The key consideration for Favor Curriers is not whether an idea is good, but whether it is acceptable and popular. The desire never to disappoint undercuts personal initiative. No pastor can work effectively in the church or among other pastors unless he or she develops the personal strength to tolerate the stress of disappointing others from time to time.

The Petty Trivialist

Petty Trivialists become obsessed with irrelevant issues or insignificant details in the political life of pastors. They consume time during important community deliberations with discussion that blurs the real issues at hand. This practice may seem harmless, but it disengages aspirations from significant social or personal issues. The preoccupation with trivialities allows detachment from ministry, insulation from confrontation and engagement, and protection from risk-taking. The ambitions of the Petty Trivialists become mired in organizational procedure or misdirected toward peripheral concerns of little consequence.

The Blissfully Sedate

Some exercise their power by abstention. These are the pastors who take little or no initiative—not so much out of unhappiness as lethargy. The Blissfully Sedate are happy with what takes the least effort. Unwilling to study the issues or participate in debate, their unambitious approach to community life saps energy from the whole group. And often their church leadership reflects these same qualities. They look for excuses to cut back on work. They report feeling bored, but never admit their own complicity in that condition. They change Wesley's "leisure and I have taken leave" to "industry and I have taken leave."

The Arbitrary Intervener

The ambition of Arbitrary Interveners takes them into places they are not needed and business that is not theirs. They squelch the talents of other pastors and staff through ill-timed and unnecessary interventions. Believing themselves to be experts in every realm, every program must have their fingerprints; every project must be shaped by their opinions and decisions. They equate success with coercing others to view things as they do.

The Ideological Fanatic

The ambitions of Ideological Fanatics flow through one single canal. With only one issue to press, they push their cause in every possible setting, whether or not it is germane and appropriate. Every stage and every meeting provides an opportunity to score points for their single issue. Abortion, pacifism, pornography, church growth, evangelicalism, the environment—the opportunities for single-issue platforms extend across the theological and political spectrum.

Destruction of Community

The above list of political pastors points directly to the undercurrents and manipulations that pastors find revolting in ministry.

The caricatures do not represent people so much as conversations, occasions, and encounters that all of us have experienced with our colleagues, and within ourselves. They describe you and me, but fortunately, very few of us are dominated by them. It is more likely that pastors who are otherwise genuine may slip into one of these modes, and for a few moments say more than anyone needs to hear (the Rumor Monger) or let some inappropriate selfish insistence surface (the Self-seeker).

But whether characteristic of some of us all the time, or of all of us some of the time, the destructive effects on our ministry are incalculable.

This kind of politics poisons community life. Playing any of the above roles makes it difficult to be genuine in relationship with others. Other pastors become stepping stones or stumbling blocks. Political pastors use their colleagues as sources of information or as votes to be tabulated, but cannot appreciate the mutuality of ministry. When a gathering of pastors becomes a cauldron of competing self-interests, unspeaking rivalries, and internal antagonisms, we forfeit the blessings of community. Naked aggression replaces boldness for Christ.

Such politically minded pastors project their motives onto everyone else. They assume that everyone who succeeds in ministry has done so by political shrewdness and cunning, rather than by recognized ability and commitment. They politicize every action. The pastor who hosts the guest speaker is seen as solicitous; the pastor who speaks in favor of a supervisor's point of view is posturing; the pastor who shows pictures of a new mission project is suspected of having a calculated plan for personal advancement. No act is so innocent that sagacious minds cannot regard it as self-serving.

The Politics of Manipulation

Are these characteristics overdrawn? Meet David. During my first year in seminary, I heard about David, who had been there several years before. He was someone who luxuriated in the politics of ministry. He loved the game of it. About once a week, when David joined a group for supper, his only topic of conversation would be clergy politics. He knew the salary of every minister in the conference and could speak for hours about strategies for "success" in ministry. Like a football fanatic who knows all the players by heart and twenty-five years of Super Bowl statistics, he could recount pastors, their stories, their successes and failures.

According to David, seminarians need to begin early to work out someone to serve their field service with: "Choose a pastor on the way up, perhaps one who will be a bishop. Choose the right church, one that has lay people who will help you later." When ministers visited seminary, David talked about which ones to be seen with and which to avoid. He had a political strategy for every situation.

David would talk about the importance of grabbing power early. He described means for manipulating the process for larger appointments and negotiating a higher salary with church boards. He described ways to leapfrog over other ministers on the way to the top.

"Never stay more than three years in one place," he would say, "or you'll be forgotten by the system."

It was said that David had ten thousand fiendishly ingenious strategies for wrangling a better placement. He particularly liked stories of ferocious and cunning victories by pastors climbing to the top, but he also enjoyed telling about naive pastors who bit the dust because of their failure of will. He mused about which titles are most important and where to get the easiest "D. Min." degree.

"Build a network of alliances so that decision makers will know some pressure as they consider your placement."

Apparently David genuinely believed that all pastors who progressed in ministry knew and practiced these secrets. It was not skill or commitment that made for meaningful ministry; it was cunning and shrewdness.

I am told that David still serves churches and still talks the same language, with the same enthusiasm. The fact that his strategies failed to work has not dampened his faith in them.

When I learned about David, it evoked a tumult of contradictory emotions in me. On the one hand, I felt it was tragic when someone willfully swims away from the lifeboat. On the other hand, I recall feeling the strange fear that David might be right, that maybe it always does matter who you know and who knows you.

I thought that if I remained faithful and did my work well, God would use me, and I would find happiness. But then I'd picture myself thirty years afterward, the forgotten pastor of a distant desert outpost, just inches this side of the end of the world, with David as my bishop! What if David was right? What if that was the way "successful" ministers thought and conspired?

Someone like David, with his unharnessed ambitions and intense self-seeking, would make Linda self-conscious about her appropriate self-assertion. David would see Linda as no different from himself, just less practiced. And David wouldn't know what to make of Mark. To him, Mark would seem extremely naive. As for Mark, he despairs over pastors like David, but refuses to let them shape his ministry.

The Politics of Resignation

Bruce hates all politics with a passion and fears any action that might make him look self-seeking. He is so afraid of being David that he cannot experience satisfaction in ministry, as Linda does.

Bruce takes no initiative. He knows there is a political realm to community life in ministry, but he steadfastly refuses to play any of its games.

Political talk causes Bruce to feel left out; it makes David feel like an insider. David loves politics in the church as much as Bruce hates it.

Bruce does not speak freely with his supervisors for fear of seeming to be promoting himself. He goes through periods when he feels forgotten by the system, mistreated by a process that focuses on the more aggressive pastors around him.

Over the years, Bruce has developed a theology to sustain his passivity, believing it is wrong to assert himself ambitiously. To his peers, his lack of self-assertion springs more from a problem with authority than from a sound personal ethic.

At times, Bruce's theology becomes so skewed by his feelings that he begins to suspect that anyone who is successful in ministry will compromise the mission of the church. A smouldering cynicism burns inside him. Bruce has a good mix of gifts for ministry, but he cannot express his needs or the needs of his family to his supervisors.

Securing the Boundaries

To restore a sense of community to our political life, we must temper our exercise of power and redirect our ambitions in ways that build up community, rather than destroy it.

Mutual Examination

Paul writes, "Examine yourselves to see whether you are living in the faith. Test yourselves" (II Cor. 13:5). To avoid the destructive temptations of politics in ministry effectively requires a constant and deliberate effort to reevaluate and shape our intentions.

We do not choose our motives. Motives pounce upon us as uncontrolled emotions and impulses which act on our wills. On the other hand, intentions are our conscious decisions, or choices, about what we propose to do through our actions. We choose our intentions.[3]

For instance, we may intend to start a new program to help low-income families, an action founded upon our commitment to an ideal. Our efforts to influence people and to gather support are inspired and shaped by our intention.

While creating the new program, other desires and impulses may come into consciousness: "If this project succeeds, maybe I will be better known and somehow rewarded for my work. Perhaps people will start paying more attention to me than to Pastor Susan, who always gets the credit." These motives—whispers of the mind and temptations of the heart—slip upon us without our calling them forth. They spring up uninvited, entering our thoughts and occasionally influencing our actions. Their mixed quality embarrasses the sensitive spirit.

Mixed motives are best kept at bay with clear intentions, founded upon solid commitments to action. When such uninvited motives grow to the status and strength of intentions, then we are in trouble. We fall into Self-seeking and Credit Grabbing.

Paul said, "Examine yourselves." His use of the plural is provocative. He's not calling for self-examination. He is encouraging us to open ourselves to the correction of community.

"What do I really wish to accomplish? Why am I seeking this position? Do my actions arise from my intention to follow Christ, or are they inspired by my need to show people my competence?" These are the questions we need to ask ourselves about our political involvements in ministry. We also need to invite our closest companions in ministry to ask these questions of us. In our Christian sisters and brothers, when we trust them enough to invite their probing questions, we can find the Christ who judges and corrects, comforts and encourages.

Appropriate Means

In the politics of ministry, the way we pursue our objectives bears a witness just as powerful as the objectives we choose to pursue.

When we refer to appropriate means, we include the open, honest, full participation of people. Much behind-the-scenes politicking betrays a lack of trust in the wider community. The last thing we should fear in the church is that the truth will get out.

The cornerstone of any volunteer agency is self-disclosure and public participation. People want to know why certain actions have been taken, who makes decisions, where their money goes. They want their voices heard. Any process that devalues these impulses undermines the witness of the organization.

The cornerstone of covenantal ministry is carved by love, trust, mutuality. While we need not make public everything we say in private, we should act in such a way that if our actions and discussions become public, we have no cause for embarrassment. To the extent that we are honest with others, we probably will be more honest with ourselves. Such honesty helps us harness destructive politicking.

Poisoning the Well

Poisoning the well refers to those practices that pour unnecessary garbage into community debate, to cloud rather than clarify. Such tactics falsely and intensely exacerbate differences rather than resolve issues.

Calling refugee workers "communists" or those opposed to refugee work "unChristian" is poisoning the well. Calling pro-choice people "abortionists" and pro-life people "fanatics" does not open dialogue. Calling someone "racist"—not because the epithet fits, but to further one's purposes—poisons the well. Pointing out an opponent's moral failings that are irrelevant to the issue being debated poisons the well. By such tactics, we do immeasurable harm to our brothers and sisters, and to our witness together.

A Level Playing Field

Imagine elevating one end of a football field thirty feet higher than the other. One team would have all the momentum of gravity to its advantage, while the other would wear itself out running uphill on each play.

Too often in church politics, those with all the advantages do not seek a level playing field, but remain satisfied with the preferments they enjoy, while those running uphill would rather have an opportunity to play from the higher turf than seek a level field. If we are to take seriously our mutuality in ministry, our only meaningful goal is a level playing field, neither enjoying nor feeling victimized by special preferments.

Some male pastors know, without a doubt, that a particular church will not consider any of their female colleagues of equal talent and experience for the role of senior pastor. Rather than question this advantage, many male pastors accept it as an unsolicited benefit which they find counter-productive to deny. Our covenant demands more of us.

What tilts the playing field? One person has information to which others do not have access; decisions are made without full participation; accepted processes are circumvented; openings are filled before they are announced; a position is awarded on the basis of friendship with the decision makers; candidates are excluded because of race or sex.

Covenant demands that we ask ourselves questions of intention. Are we each seeking only to have *our* claims fulfilled? Or do we seek to be treated fairly, to receive equal consideration with others?

Probing the question of fairness guards against, or at least reins in, the two most dangerous components in our political relationships—stealth and self-interest.

Whom We Serve

"Most people, if given the choice between having a better world, or a better place within the world as it is, would choose the latter." That pessimistic view of human motivation came from Ralph Sockman more than thirty years ago. When we substitute the word *denomination* for *world*, do we agree with this assessment for pastors?

Every day we face the decision of whom we serve. Do we work for ourselves or for the gospel? Is our goal to put the right minister in a certain position, or is it to put ourselves in that position, whether we're right for it or not?

To offer serious theological correctives to our political life, we must give constant consideration to whom we serve. In covenant, we ask that question of others, and we invite others to ask it of us. We work with a basic and fearful trust in the accountability to which we are held by our brothers and sisters. Our trust is basic, because we cannot live faithfully and act truthfully without it. It is fearful, because, in the redemptive work of community, some of our lower motivations come to light.

A Fundamental Duplicity

As Christian ministers, sensitive to the impulses of our own spirits, we must accept the tension between self-giving and self-serving, between personal pursuits and service in Christ's name. We handle the tension more genuinely and constructively when we do not deny it or evade it.

Albert Camus, in *The Fall*, writes, "After prolonged research on myself, I brought out the fundamental duplicity of the human being. Then I realized that modesty helped me to shine, humility to conquer, and virtue to oppress." Moth-to-flame political ambitions pose the greatest threat to those no longer aware of this inner tension.

The heart of ethical struggle is pitting one ethical value against another. For instance, our commitment to truth may lead us to one action, while the value of loyalty takes us in another direction. If we know that a friend in ministry is doing something destrucive, we carefully weigh how we use the information we have. We may lift loyalty above truth, if we believe that the consequence of revealing our information would be out of portion to the offense. Or we may lift truth above loyalty, if we feel the infringement is grave enough to inform the proper supervisor. Reconciling our competing values leads to integrity and genuine growth.

But we are not allowed to pit an ethical value against an unethical one. The struggle between truth and success, between loyalty and greed, should be no struggle at all. Weighing whether to leave the wrong impression in order to fulfill selfish appetites, or considering whether to hurt a colleague in order to gain advantage—these are not ethical struggles, but skirmishes with temptation, wars between the two armies of our own duplicity.

Handling the duplicity of our own souls means that we let our intentions, rather than our selfish impulses, form our actions. In service to Christ, we say, "Here, take some of mine," while thinking, "I wish I had all of yours," trusting that this is not loss of self, but the first step toward the recovery of self.

FOR PERSONAL REFLECTION OR GROUP DISCUSSION

◇

What fears or unmet needs feed the ambitions of Mathematical Magicians, Rumor Mongers, and Influence Peddlers? What changes in the personal lives of pastors, or in our community life together, might reduce the destructiveness of some of these forces?

◇

Do the caricatures in this chapter (Influence Peddlers, etc.) represent tendencies you see among pastors? Do you find yourself occasionally falling into any of these modes of thought and speech?

◊

Consider a pastor you admire deeply for her or his integrity and effectiveness. How has this person dealt with the politics of ministry constructively? How does this person exercise power positively?

◊

How do you respond to the political side of denominational life? How is your effectiveness shaped by the politics of ministry? What tempers your exercise of power?

◊

What suggestions might you have for our political life together that would relieve some of the destructive elements of the politics of ministry while enhancing the positive?

◊

CHAPTER SIX

Accountable and Complete

The Gift of Living for Others

Sometimes we are ambitious "for me and for more." At other times, we strive to serve God. There are unattractive aspects of our souls that we do not care to visit. Yet their power over us remains strongest when they are invisible. The first step toward strengthening positive ambition and harnessing unhealthy ambition is to recognize that we harbor the capacity for both. By granting definition to our destructive impulses, we lift them from mist and haze to tamable proportion.

Just as responsible drinkers of alcohol must watch the boundaries so that their habit does not become addictive, perhaps career-conscious ministers need to admit, "I must watch my ambitions. I could easily drag my family across the state every two years, chasing the shadows of my soul, pursuing higher salaries and larger churches."

When the tensions are recognized, accepted, and befriended, they foster authenticity in ministry and stimulate spiritual growth. As we balance opposing tendencies within ourselves, they begin to work for us; they lose their power to diminish our fruitfulness, our fulfillment, our mutuality.

Mutuality or Competition

The New Testament suggests a model for community, the mutual sharing of material goods and spiritual gifts (Acts

2:44-47). We love, worship, serve, and witness in community, and toward the goal of community.

Having "all things in common" was not just a material arrangement, a sharing of goods, but also a spiritual relationship. We have one another in common. Rather than each of us playing a single role with our individual functions, in *koinonia* we participate in the ministries of one another.

You are present in what I do, and I in what you do. I am part of your ministry, and you are part of mine, because we are both part of Christ. I am accountable for your well-being, as you are for mine. In mutuality, we share one another's burdens, delight in one another's successes, and offer ourselves fully in service to one another. We call one another to greater fullness. It is not you *against* me, *instead* of me, *under* me, or *over* me. It is you *in service* to me, and I to you, both of us thereby expressing our service to Christ.

Koinonia is the harvest for which we till the soil. We strive to deepen community for the sake of God's reign. God's intention for community was made known to us in a decisive way through Jesus Christ, in whom God was "reconciling the world to himself" (II Cor. 5:19).

When we live for others and not for ourselves, we are on the road to full personhood.

> As long as we try to erect self-worth on the basis of what I alone can do . . . we fall back into an essentially individualistic or egocentric way of thinking. . . . The miracle of mutuality is that while loving the other, one discovers that one is being loved by the other in the same way. Without intending one's own affirmation, one finds oneself affirmed because that is the meaning of mutuality: two persons loving each other create through the mutuality of their love the worth and dignity of each.[1]

Self-worth is mutual, not individual. As *koinonia* forms our intentions toward our brothers and sisters in ministry, it offers the most profound answer to destructive ambitions. It guides us toward those personal contributions that lead to the fulfillment of our personality, not to its diminution.

Aimed at *koinonia,* we work just as hard as before, but we are clear that our goal is not to serve the highest steeple in the land or to outdo everyone else. Not only are our spiritual and emotional needs for community met with new depth, but our individual expressions and impulses are encouraged and developed.

By the laying on of hands, the church has aimed us toward community. Jesus prayed, "As you, Father, are in me and I am in you, may they also be in us . . . . The glory that you have given me I have given them, so that they may be one, as we are one, I in them and you in me, that they may become completely one" (John 17:21-23).

In ordination, we enter a relationship of mutuality with other pastors. *Koinonia* is our highest ambition. We work for it and pray for it. We teach it, encourage it, strengthen it, and we should exemplify it in our relations with other clergy.

What is *koinonia* like among pastors? We delight again in communion, association, close relationship. We are unashamed to use our gifts while desiring the best for others. Rather than bolster our own records, we strengthen one another through times of vulnerability. We learn from others' courage and risk, from others' fears and struggles, from our hesitations, false starts, and victories. We view church placement less as competition and more as a creative process which requires our honesty and humility. We pray for one another through all the disturbances and triumphs of ministry. Our covenant with one another helps us fulfill our covenant with God.

Mutuality helps us distinguish God-given goals from culturally conditioned ones. It means seriously altering our reward systems to reflect our mutuality. We eliminate as much as possible the divisive and competitive issues that surround salary, by restraining the extremes of poverty and excess. We find, in the closeness of Christian collegiality, a place where we can share significantly without fear of being exploited or embarrassed.

So much of our ministerial conduct is ceremonial kindness, a conventional solicitude. The absence of community looms between us. The yearning of isolated souls goes unnoticed, or at least unspoken. Our capacity to grow and learn is directly linked to our ability to break through the barriers to initiate and nurture relationships.

I am a pastor, and I know how difficult *koinonia* is among pastors. We support so many false images of ministry. We dream of the pastor able to beat back troubles with clear and cunning victories. Instead, most pastors feel nearly powerless in today's world. We picture the friendly pastor, surrounded by love. Instead, most pastors, even in supportive congregations, feel desperately lonely. The personal isolation of the pastor is a recurring theme in issues of clergy morale, family break-ups, vocational distress, promiscuity, and alcohol abuse.

And each of us supports illusions about our own abilities—that we are somehow better than other pastors or more deserving, or that we are the overlooked and ignored. These false images foster our individualistic impulses.

Koinonia tests our images in the confessional presence of others. It is not simply a nice family feeling, but a tough mutuality that confronts and challenges, to help us reach out and extend our ministries to the full extent of our capacities. *Koinonia* is a mutual inner resource with an outward focus. We discover that we are not alone, but are able to complete someone else's competencies for ministry, and must depend upon others to complete ours. *Koinonia* takes us as close as we can come to the Christ who judges, corrects, and blesses us to new life. Community sets us free from cultural expectations and selfish ambitions. It represents the reality behind all our illusions, which we must regain, so that we become servants of Christ rather than slaves to culture.

Deitrich Bonhoeffer, in *Life Together*, reminds us that an incomparable joy results from the physical presence of other Christians. We see "in the companionship of a fellow Christian a physical sign of the gracious presence of Christ." In community, the Christian no longer seeks "his justification in himself, but in Jesus Christ alone."[2]

According to Bonhoeffer, every Christian needs another Christian when she or he becomes uncertain and discouraged.

The Christ in one's own heart is weaker than the Christ in the word of a brother or sister.

The more genuine and deeper our community, the more everything else between us recedes. Community is not an ideal which we must realize, but a reality created by God, in which we may participate. The key question is not, "Is *koinonia* possible among pastors?" but rather, "How do we participate in it today?"

Autonomy or Individualism

Unharnessed individualism breeds too much selfish insistence and fosters aggressive "me first" ambitions. It is empty self-assertion, unsustained by compassion, community, or love-determined goals. It creates isolation, mistrust, and resentment, and works against the possibility of mutuality.

In contrast to individualism, we have *autonomy*, the capacity for a healthy balance between independence and interdependence. John Harris offers a helpful discussion about the importance of autonomy in pastors' relationship with congregations. Autonomy is also important in relation to placement systems and supervisors.[3]

Harris defines autonomy as the inner ability to govern ourselves. It is the capacity to balance and resolve opposing demands within ourselves and between ourselves and others. We break free from the fear that comes with feeling overdependent on the institution, as if the placement system and our supervisors have the power to decide whether we shall live happily and fruitfully or not. Autonomous pastors enjoy an inner confidence that allows them to risk and grow and provide fruitful and challenging ministry without an overriding fear of failure or disapproval.

Unlike individualism, autonomy does not create socially isolated pastors, but gives us the capacity for inner direction in the company of the others we are called to serve, the ability to hold in tension a clear sense of our primary needs and the primary needs of the community. Autonomy frees us from psychic captivity to the placement system, the approval of our parishioners, and the culturally sustained perceptions of career advancement. We work more from inner choice, freely made, than from external necessity. We arrive at a point where personal fulfillment no longer relies on successfully courting approbation, nor does it depend entirely upon professional advancement. It is found in living out the purposes of Christ.

Sometimes we work out of a desperate love of ourselves. We want to form the church in our image. We become so identified with our congregation that for it to succeed is for us to succeed; for it to fall back is for us to fail. The church becomes a reflection of ourselves. We build up the church in order to build our career.

Over-identifying with the church is a prescription for compulsive work habits and spiritual collapse. We work out of desperation, fear of failure, panic about our careers. Success is getting the church to do things our way. What we love is not the church, but ourselves. When ambitions that look so outwardly fruitful are really inwardly directed, they cannot sustain the spirit through the difficult tasks of ministry.

A "healthy disenchantment" with the church can help us maintain autonomy and keep our ambitions in balance.[4] Then we can face the imperfections of our placement system without a bitter cynicism, but with enough emotional distance to free us from the childish illusion that the system will supply all we ever need for satisfaction and self-affirmation.

We wake up to realize that our self-validation comes from somewhere other than our careers. This frees our ambitions from the narrow channels of career advancement, so that we may apply our energy and talent and reason for the purposes of Christ, rather than for personal advancement. Autonomy leads to less desperate and more authentic ministry than does individualism. With autonomy, we give our best for the church, but we don't depend upon the church for our final validation.

Autonomy does not usually demand a dramatic change in direction. Sometimes it is the emotional and spiritual *capacity* to step down, or back, or out, which provides enough distance to break the dependency, whether we exercise these options or not. To know that we *can* say *no* to advancement, that our ambitions *can* drive us elsewhere than up the ladder, grants a profound freedom that makes even our *yes* to advancement more authentic. By keeping the primary tasks in focus and channeling our ambitions toward them, we experience a healthy autonomy from the need for advancement and from the cultural pressures that would narrow the definition of success in ministry.

Honest Assessment or Self-deception

Why do clothing stores put three-way mirrors near dressing rooms? We need many different angles to get a clear sense of ourselves.

Yet when we look at ourselves in ministry, sometimes we deny ourselves the same opportunity. We are not sure that we want to know how others see us. We fear being painfully disillusioned.

Not everyone was made to serve huge churches or to supervise others. The fact that so many of us think we should provides no evidence that we are attuned to God's call; it only offers confirmation of society's powerful pressures and pride's perseverance in the saints. God has no such goals for everyone. Not everyone is an outstanding preacher; not everyone has the patience and insight for meaningful pastoral care. Harnessing our ambitions includes realistically assessing how and where we can make the biggest difference for God's purposes.

Much of the pain of ambition comes from the sharp contrast between what we *want* to do and what we are *capable* of doing. As a corrective to destructive ambition, we need to invite an accurate picture of ourselves and come to peace with our contribution to the church.

John Wesley wove together strands from various traditions to compose the Covenant Prayer:

> I am no longer mine own, but give myself to thy will in all things. . . . Put me to what thou wilt, rank me with whom thou wilt; . . . let me be employed by thee, or laid aside for thee, exalted for thee or trodden underfoot for thee; . . . let me have all things, let me have nothing.[5]

To pray those words honestly will enable us to live peacefully with the contribution we have to offer the body of Christ, without fretting that we do not offer what others do, or worrying that we do not receive what others do.

Genuine dialogue with other pastors bolsters our confidence in areas in which we have competencies we do not recognize, and humbles us when our vision of ourselves is dangerously overdrawn. By sharing our aspirations, we gain more accurate perceptions of ourselves as we study the multiple reflections in their responses. We face the Christ in our brothers and sisters, which encourages and humbles. Sometimes we confront our own complicity in the crises that our ambitions create for us.

Honest assessment means that we gracefully invite the perceptions of lay people. It is for the people of God that we do our work. If we move to another church without resolving the inconsistencies in ourselves described by the laity, we carry our classroom to the next parish, painfully extending the time it takes to master those skills or insights.

Sometimes we struggle against evaluation. We fear the disillusionment that might follow a negative evaluation. But disillusion is good if it helps us break through our illusions about ourselves. To see ourselves as others see us adds clarity and balance to our self-perceptions.

And honest assessment requires that our supervisors receive an accurate view of who we are. What matters most is not that we serve the biggest church, but that we serve the right church. If we consistently bolster our record, pretending to have competencies we do not possess, we offer a fraudulent picture. Few pastors are lonelier than those who have climbed to places of prominence on fewer abilities than they profess.

Grace with Works

Somewhere along the way, we have been given the wrong road map. We believe that what we *do* and what we *have* leads to what we *are*, that the more we *do* and the more we *have*, the more we *are*. We arrive at *being* on this map as a result of *doing* and *having*. This map is passed out freely at every magazine rack, bookstore, and cinema in the country. All our frantic *doing* and our endless appetite for *having* arise from our need to create a better *being*. Our accomplishments and acquisitions, like trusses and beams, support and sustain our sense of being.

In the book of Acts, the authorities speak with fear about the arrival of Paul and Silas: "These people who have been turning the world upside down have come here also" (17:6). Actually, Paul and Silas were turning the world right side up. They brought with them a new road map, one more true to the terrain of our souls.

Their message was simple but profound: We are what we are—not by our merits, but by the grace of Jesus Christ. We are children of God, of immeasurable worth and eternal value, loved by God. What we *do* and *have* flow from that. *Doing* and *having* are not prerequisites for being. Our work is part of the result of being, an effect of being, but not a support of being.[6] We do not work to satisfy our deepest needs; we work because our deepest needs are satisfied.

A key goal of our religious faith is that we be able to conquer our expectation of reward for our achievements. The highest ambitions in human life are not achieved for reward, but are propelled by the experience of God's grace.

When we grasp the significance of salvation by grace alone, God's Spirit flows through us, guiding us and drawing us out. It is not other peoples' things that drive us (envy), nor our own appetite (greed), nor our frustration (anger). We move with a more relaxed posture, working in joyful response because our salvation has been given to us. We find the strength to offer ourselves where we are needed, rather than where we want to go or where our culture has told us we must want to go.

When we encounter the grace that alone ends our striving, we find a purpose for life so compelling that we no longer need to compensate for the void within ourselves by seeking lesser objects of ambition. We appreciate an inner distance from the childish need to have and to do everything. Grace grants us an assurance of worth that redeems us from our sense of failure and our fear of failure. God's grace redeems us from our need to prove ourselves. Whether we feel embraced by people's love, or whether we have struggled with its painful absence, God redeems us.

Productive Work and Redemptive Rest

The idea of Sabbath is more than a day off, although that in itself is a first step. In Sabbath, we set aside our work in the world to focus on God's work in the world. We remember, in proper perspective, our ties to God and our relationship to work. A searching Sabbath keeps us from thinking that "my power and the might of my own hand have gotten me this" (Deut. 8:17).

Observing Sabbath was extremely impractical for the outcast Hebrews in the wilderness more than three thousand years ago, since survival depended upon continual work to obtain provision. Sabbath revealed a deep trust in God's grace. There the Hebrews expressed the faith that our lives will go on, even if, during one day, we don't produce. There are yearnings more important than our physical appetites.

Everyone needs time to remember that God justifies us it is not our own doing and having. We will find greater satisfaction in all our work when we experience God's acceptance. We have nothing to prove in those moments, yet we have everything to gain.

In our *giving* mode, we prepare for others, help others, listen to others. This includes study, speaking, sermon preparation, and visiting.

We also have a *busyness* mode. We shuffle papers, fix copiers, mow lawns, set up chairs. John Wesley punctuated his diaries with: "necessary business."

Sabbath reminds us of our *receiving* mode, times when we do not give or do. But this is not laziness. Sabbath may involve some of our most courageous work, as we confront some things about ourselves that we have been avoiding through our busyness.

Occasionally we let go of our productive self, the self that needs to do things, show things, compare things, compete in things, prove things, and build things. We need times for reclaiming the unadorned self, vulnerable, open to receive and give love, regardless of any accomplishments.[7] In Sabbath, Christ's most pressing question is not, "What have you accomplished?" but, "Do you love me?" (John 21:15-19).

Because pastors write on Saturdays and work on Sundays, it's an occupational hazard to lose touch with the trust that Sabbath reveals and the grace that Sabbath bestows. Ignoring Sabbath, we cling to our trust in works. We feel that we need to *do* something all the time. Our compulsion to work endless hours may be related to the poverty of our prayer life, the vagueness of our sense of purpose in ministry, the absence of any focused study and spiritual growth.

In Sabbath we become less reactive to the emotions of pride, envy, and anger that spring up uninvited in our work. Our souls return to us in Sabbath. We sustain an inner strength that helps us act competently and react with a minimum of defensiveness, less preoccupied with promotion and more focused on the purposes we serve.

Sabbath takes place during periods of reflection and reading each day, early or late, when no one needs our help. We experience it during a day of study and prayer, or a time of retreat. We need recreation, but that isn't Sabbath. Sabbath serves no purpose if we fill the day with another kind of striving. If Jesus needed times for prayer and solitude, we cannot presume that we can live fruitfully and faithfully without it.

Savoring the Victories

Unharnessed ambition robs us of our victories and steals away our satisfactions before we can enjoy them.

Some pastors preach excellent messages on Sunday morning, then rush home to begin work on the next Sunday's sermon. They do the same with youth programs and stewardship campaigns. They never enjoy the smooth taste of accomplishment before sticking their forks into something else. They dive into the next course without pausing to clear the palate. They are constantly hungry, even when surrounded by plenty.

Satisfaction in a job well done provides the spiritual

nourishment we often neglect. We can enjoy genuine praise without courting it or depending upon it.

When we leave one project to immediately immerse ourselves in the next, we overlook how deeply our work matters. Sometimes the fruit of our work seems elusive—not because the difference we make is inconsequential, but because we do not take time to notice the changes we have wrought. We rush from one field to the next sowing seed, without ever looking over our shoulder to see what has sprouted. The next project, or the next church, holds all our hope.

"Savoring our victories" means that we should luxuriate occasionally in the past rather than continually push toward the future. Paul found great pleasure in remembering his experiences. He did not fall into destructive pride over his accomplishments, but he did bask in a sense of having done well: "I have fought the good fight" (II Tim. 4:7).

When we stroll less hurriedly through life, we find more time to reflect. All of us have our experiences in ministry, though too often we have no reflections on our experiences. To savor our victories means we do not just live our experiences, but hold them and caress them occasionally, considering where they lead and what they reveal. We look for the role God plays in our work, and what theological meanings our church projects offer. We look at events and how they change us, and change the church, and change the lives of our members.

When we savor our victories, rather than glancing over letters of appreciation before throwing them away, we receive them, read them, hear their truth, and accept their grace. This is not overindulgence. Such words are meant as gifts. Too often, we shrug off words of gratitude without letting their balm soothe and strengthen us. We need not depend upon them, but we need not discard them as untruthful. This helps us sense the accomplishments that other people see in us.

Savoring our victories leads to dramatic changes in our sense of ministry. We find ourselves serving longer pastorates. Many pastors feel that they have accomplished little, simply because they haven't stayed in one place long enough to see their sowing come to harvest. The fruit of an effective children's program takes years to ripen. How tragic that few pastors see those children who received their ministry grow into responsible adolescents.

In the book of Acts, we see slivers of activity sliced from the decades and condensed into a few short pages. We lose sight of the span of years. We see little of the long marches along barren roads, the months of ship travel and tent-making between the occasions for ministry. We read the exceptional victories in quick succession.

During the low points, the early church kept its vision alive and its faith vibrant by retelling the high points. It relived the victories, not to boast, but to celebrate. The early Christians recovered their identity each time they retold the story of the day of Pentecost, of Peter's clashes with authority and Paul's encounter with Christ on the way to Damascus. We need to savor our victories so that during the in-between times, we can continue our work in faithfulness.

Sharing in a Community of Faith

Pastors are immersed in community from the first sip of coffee at the prayer breakfast until we lock the last door after choir rehearsal.

Yet we frequently experience community only from the position of leadership. We seldom worship without feeling responsible for something. Even in the most casual gathering at the church, our eyes catch the light bulb that needs replacing and our ears detect noises in the air conditioner.

We study the Bible far more frequently because of our ordination than because of our baptism. We offer far more prayers because we are pastors than because we are Christians. We perform so many of our functions profession- ally that we often lead a community of faith without really feeling a part of it. In a painful irony, pastors can stand essentially alone in a faith whose purpose is community.

Pastors need a community of faith. Our real church is that small, intimate gathering composed of whatever little group in Christ we are able to trust. These friends bring us Christ's judgment and comfort. Such a personal church helps to shape our destructive ambitions into life-giving aspirations.

Without community, no one senses the sloughs into which we slip, and no one reaches in to pull us out. Both our victories and our failures accentuate our loneliness. Only in the embrace of community can we feel sustained by the everlasting arms of God.

Our leadership in our local church makes receiving more difficult than giving. When we do attend worship from the pews, often a critical voice inside us overpowers the speakers in front of us. We notice their gestures and inflections. We wonder where they got their ideas, and we think about how we would say it differently. We cannot set aside our professional ears long enough to hear God speak to us.

And we have trouble finding community because we do not know our clergy brothers and sisters well enough or see them frequently enough for our lives to intermingle to the depths of our faith.

In one urban area, several pastors meet to attend Saturday night services at a nondenominational church. Other pastors attend spiritual formation retreats. Some meet regularly with other clergy for prayer or study. The grace of *koinonia* often requires our initiative.

A Ministry of Encouragement

In *koinonia*, pastors work as priests to one another, not as competitive marketers of the same product. Our assemblies are more than interdepartmental powwows to learn the newest sales techniques. To discover community among pastors, we must work for it, build on it, and celebrate when it appears. Intentionality is crucial.

Paul sprinkles his letters with "encouragement": "Therefore encourage one another and build up each other"; "Encourage the faint hearted" (I Thess. 5:11, 14).

We embrace *koinonia* through a ministry of encouragement, each to the other. We help one another combat the discouragement that comes from faltering programs, poor responses, congregational intransigence, dispiriting antagonism. We listen to career aspirations and share professional disappointments. We offer and receive support through family entanglements.

And we give one another courage to try new things, to challenge prevailing norms when appropriate, to risk growth. We give mutual permission to expand into new interests.

All of us enjoy an unmistakable satisfaction when we are recognized for our contribution by being advanced in position. But no matter how rapid our ascension or how neglected by the process we may feel, our clergy placement systems never promote us satisfactorily enough to feed our need for self-assurance. When the only reward we can experience for our work is a larger church, we become frustrated and apathetic, working at the lowest levels of energy. Many pastors experience periods of personal panic when they come to a plateau in career ascendancy.

The ministry of encouragement helps us fill some of our hungers without the need for constant advancement. To hear from our sisters and brothers that they genuinely value our ministry provides a balm for our wounded ambitions and starves some of the resentments we might otherwise nourish. Through mutual encouragement and by cultivating deeper friendships, we provide one another with "promotions" more enduring than simple advancement.

Conversations that ramble on about salaries and pastoral moves deplete our spirits. We feel parched by the barrenness of competition. When pastors overflow with cynicism about the church and slosh around in their self-serving appetites, we feel disheartened.

On the other hand, we find ourselves reinvigorated by conversations that express our hopes and fears, that require close listening and mutual sharing. These refresh us. Our boasting separates us, but our vulnerabilities draw us closer.

We influence an atmosphere of mutuality in a gathering of pastors when we direct conversations away from the exterior measures of ministry. We genuinely inquire about each other's families. The intentional cultivation of friendship comes from time together, the intermingling of our families, and perhaps a self-imposed banishment of success stories.

The Rumor Mongers, the Mathematical Magicians, and all their friends stand as a spiritual demolition crew in every gathering of pastors. The ministry of encouragement works in the opposite direction. It edifies. By building one another up in love, we give visible evidence of *koinonia*.

Sometimes we need to avoid the people who evoke in us a sense of envy, competition, and anger, if they only step up our discontent. But if we can see through their braggadocio to their essential hunger, then perhaps we can remain strong enough to offer them the ministry of encouragement. They may not know how their actions distance them from the refreshing friendship they thirst for.

One pastor practices the ministry of encouragement through notes and letters. He began the habit as a battle against his own discouragement. This is no strategy to win friends and influence people; he solicits no votes. He offers genuine concern, congratulating pastors on family occasions and commenting on creative accomplishments in the church.

On my first Sunday in my first pastorate, as I trembled toward the door to leave for church, the phone rang. A pastor I only knew as an acquaintance called to say that he was thinking about me and hoped everything would go well, that nervousness was natural. His call made a significant difference to me.

Pastors who serve small churches sometimes feel spun to the periphery. Churches that don't grow tend to fall from the front pages of our concern. We need to care more deeply for one another. Our brothers and sisters need our support. It is Christ's ministry they are doing, so it is ours too.

Pastors who serve large churches also need our help. Many have enjoyed an overabundance of secondary and tertiary accomplishments. But they risk losing touch with the primary tasks of ministry as much as anybody. The circle of conversation for some has shrunk to their own staff members. They may feel too busy to take time for other pastors. And frequently, their success has been met with ostracism and envy. *Koinonia* inspires us to bring them back with a ministry of encouragement.

In a church-growth atmosphere, powerful preaching is more

valued and visible than pastoral care, evangelism is noticed more than ministries to the terminally ill, visitation to the unchurched receives more praise than visitation to the homebound. This creates a host of specialized pastors who receive little recognition. Our regard for those who feel overlooked shows that we believe their ministries are extensions of ours, and ours of theirs.

Life, Faith, and Career

We have a life. We have a faith. We have a calling as a pastor. Sometimes these take us in the same direction, smoothly humming like a well-tuned machine. At other times, they take us in different directions, and as with tires out of alignment, we feel every bump and pull and jolt.

Each of us has a life. We have the joys and responsibilities that come with families. We have our personal interests and hobbies. Perhaps we take our public involvements seriously in the arena of politics and community service.

In life, as in our pastoral callings, we have a God-given responsibility to use ourselves fully. Life goals include the kind of marriage we would like, the physical health we would like to enjoy, the books we would like to read, the places we'd like to see.

I know one pastor who lives for his archeological visits to the Middle East every few years, and another whose concern for the environment centers on birds—she travels everywhere to observe them and photograph them. Another pastor studies Spanish with a private tutor, for his enjoyment rather than for his job.

Our life goals also include our involvement in our families, the lives and careers of our spouses, the hobbies we develop together.

Some pastors need a life outside their office and away from their sanctuary. Without collar and robe, each is first a person. We pursue these *life* ambitions without frantic efforts to prove our capabilities. They grant us reprieve and perspective from our work.

And we have our faith. It came to us with our baptism and

called us to ministry—first the general ministry and later to ordination. Our faith moves us to do things and learn things that even our pastoral careers do not call out of us.

One group of pastors began to rethink the issue of clergy salaries. Troubled by the deep discrepancies among clergy, they each quietly pledged a certain amount of their own money, apart from their tithe to the church, to a general fund, to be drawn upon by pastors in need of medical care or educational expenses for their children. They did this in response to the promptings of their faith; they did not do it to further their own careers.

Another group of pastors organized to carry out projects in areas in need of better housing. They had worked on such projects from a leadership position among laity. Led by their faith, they volunteered their own time, apart from their professional role.

Our faith aspirations aim us toward capacities we would like to develop in our spiritual lives, perhaps apart from our pastoral office. It was our faith that gave us the inner ears through which we heard our call to ministry. When we began, our success and work in the ministry *resulted from* our faith commitment.

Painfully, many of us have discovered that now our faith has come to rest on success and hard work. Sometimes when pastors retire, they discover that since they no longer preach and teach and pray in public, they have no private faith. When our work fails, our faith flounders. We need to retrieve our faith from the clutches of careerism.

And then we have our callings and careers. The ambitions we pursue in this realm often include our hope for more significant outreach. Most of us also keep an eye open for advancement.

We express healthy ambitions when our career aspirations are informed by our faith goals and balanced by our life goals. Unfortunately, sometimes our career aspirations propel us forward with such momentum that we nudge our faith goals out of the way and abandon our life goals as unnecessary weight. The wheels begin to wobble, and we pay no attention to the warning signs until we've swerved clear off the road.

It is possible to live fully and develop our faith deeply while still passionately pursuing our calling. We don't need to sacrifice our ambitious energies to experience God's gracious gifts. Rather than chasing after those things that separate us from our colleagues, isolate us from our families, and poison our faith, we can find the grace that helps us enjoy life as full people, sustained by community, alive in mutuality, finding our source and end in the God who created us.

FOR PERSONAL REFLECTION OR GROUP DISCUSSION

◇

What makes gathering with other clergy appealing and enjoyable to you? On the other hand, what makes clergy gatherings difficult or uncomfortable? What conversations make you uneasy, fearful, or angry? What conversations refresh you and encourage you? What makes time together with other pastors positive—the topic, the setting, the tone, the mutual sharing, or something else?

◇

What does it take to break through conventional solicitude to reach a real mutuality at a gathering of pastors? What kind of intentionality does *koinonia* require from pastors? From supervisors?

◇

Who comprises your own personal church, those people whose trust, encouragement, and love bring you Christ's comfort and correction? Who are your most intimate and supportive companions in your spiritual life? What other pastors know your deepest aspirations? Your deepest fears? How frequently do you enjoy their presence? Have you experienced the mutuality of *koinonia* in clergy relationships? How can you strengthen those relationships?

◊

Consider an example of encouragement you have received from another pastor. What was going on in your life that made that moment memorable? How did it influence your spirit or your ministry?

◊

How is the goal of autonomy different from individualism in ministry? Describe an incident in ministry that reveals a healthy autonomy.

◊

How do you practice Sabbath? Is the time you spend in Sabbath sufficient for your spiritual needs at this point in your ministry?

◊

What professional goals do you have for the next ten years? What personal or family goals do you have? What goals do you hold for shaping your relationship with other clergy? Are any of these goals naturally exclusive of the others? How do you manage the tension?

Epilogue

Always Excelling . . .

The pastor's sudden death surprised us all. Even though he was edging toward retirement, he had seemed too young for this moment. A host of lay people and a gallery of pastors gathered to hear a succession of kindred clergy highlight our friend's service. They listed the churches he had served and reminisced upon characteristic moments selected from rich relationships that spanned the decades.

We gave thanks to God and sang "For All the Saints" with a vigor appropriate to the hymn's words. Hearts heavy with grief, we greeted the pastor's widow and met his adult daughters, with their own children clinging to their skirts. Pastors mingled with pastors. Firm handshakes, spontaneous embraces, occasional laughter, the wiping of tears, and then each of us returned to our churches to continue our work.

Thirty minutes of reminiscence and thanksgiving cannot encompass a pastor's life. Our friend had served churches for more than thirty years. If only we could measure the despair lifted and guilt relieved, the hope restored and friendships sustained, the marriages revived and youths redeemed through his faithful work. The lives touched by him are incalculable—how many sickbed hands he held in prayer, how many human wills he pushed to new resolve, how many minds he enlivened with the imponderables of our faith, how many hearts he molded with love.

His weddings and funerals and baptisms fill church records, but no book could contain all the Sunday school classes, women's groups, prayer meetings, Bible studies, youth retreats, and board meetings shaped by his spirit and mind. Even such a list would not include the quiet conversations in hospital hallways, the intimate asides at picnics, the late night prayers over telephone lines, the tender embraces when no words were appropriate. Our brother left his fingerprints upon the souls of thousands.

But now death has come to him, as eventually to all of us.

What is the place of our striving in ministry? With less ambition, our friend's circle of influence might have been half as large. His energetic pursuit of service, his conscientious manner that led to late night sermon rewrites, his taste for excellence—these blessed his life, and through them, he served the Lord.

We wrestle with the mystery that the same energies of the soul that propel us to great service can send us spinning off the road. When we turn our ambitions back on ourselves and away from community, our circle of influence for the gospel shrinks to insignificance. Lonely for the families we have neglected and cut off from the community we have disregarded, we seek a happiness that eludes our grasping.

In each pastor is replicated, in small letters, the capital challenges of the centuries. The history of the church consists of successive excursions from the same starting point—the call, periods of doubt and times of hope, the need for community and the search to stand out, our desires for spiritual gifts and earthly goods, the shaping of our ambitions by both appetite and altruism. Each of us exercises skill and persistence to overcome, solve, and serve. Each of us seeks to create more than we consume, to give more than we have received. In the story of each of us is written the history of our faith.

God has poured into our lives the same motives of countless generations, aspiring through the ages to great service. We forge our ministry in the tension between our desire to serve others and our drive to serve ourselves.

We can so easily misdirect the energies of the soul that we

call ambition. On our better days we know that our purpose is not acclaim, and it is not to outdo all the others. Our purpose is community; it is fidelity to our calling; it is evidence of lives changed—spirits comforted, hearts freed for love, minds open to the workings of grace.

If you or I were to die today, in seven years we would be remembered with fondness. Our families and friends would still feel the pain of our parting.

In seventy years, we would be a dim memory in the minds of very few, a name over a short line on a genealogy chart.

Seven hundred years from now, there would be no trace of our names on any surviving civic or church record. No tombstone could be found to list us.

Seven thousand years from now, there may be no record even of the 250-million-member society of which we are part. And yet seven thousand years is like a drop in the endless ocean of time.

When we contemplate such thoughts, a cold trickle of fear winds through our souls. We sense fully the weight of our earthly substance, our affinity with the dust from which we were formed. What is the place of our toil and striving?

Pastors die. Every pastor dies. After striving to their fullest, pushing, living, competing, pouring themselves into their work, they die. We touch thousands of lives, then the earth reclaims us all—our passions, our hopes, our fears, our failings. But one generation later, or at most two, no earthly memory remains of our work.

The fact is starkly simple: Our striving and achievements are unable to protect us from the ultimate reality that we do die and that all our works do follow us.

Perhaps it was while wrestling with the all-consuming power of death that these words were written: "All is vanity . . . what gain do they have from toiling for the wind?" (Eccl. 1:2*b*; 5:16). Or these: "As for mortals, their days are like grass; they flourish like a flower of the field; for the wind passes over it, and it is gone, and its place knows it no more" (Ps. 103:15-16).

In response, we can surrender to the bitter cynicism that life has no meaning, that all our ambitions are empty and all our work without purpose or consequence. Like ants mindlessly carrying their burdens, we fulfill our small roles until we die. Or we eat, drink, and are merry, not caring about the character of our striving.

Or we could fall into hopelessness, shrinking back in desperate and paralyzing fear, huddling over our capacities, terrified that we might use them up too soon. Fear turns us in upon ourselves.

Or we can cry out at the unfairness, the inherent injustice that turns life and work to sand and bone, that brings minds and achievements to dust.

That's the sting of death. If our significance derives from what we do, then what happens when we realize that our works do not have the power to outlive us, that they too are swallowed up in death?

But thanks be to God who gives us the victory! The significance of our lives cannot be fully expressed by what we do, what we achieve, or whether we are remembered. Certainly our value cannot be measured by how much higher some climb than others, or how much salary we earn.

Life finds its value from beyond our earthly lives, or not at all. We enjoy an imputed righteousness that is not earned or achieved. All of us are loved enough for Christ to die for us. Confrontation with our own mortality swings us full around to the necessity of grace. Meaning and purpose are not created by us, but received by us; not dependent upon our works, but accepted by our faith. The purpose of life comes from beyond ourselves. The value of our lives, whether we die young or old, infirm or productive, comes gift-like from God alone. Our ultimate significance grows out of the life, death, and resurrection of Jesus Christ.

Life is too short, our earthly frame too fragile, to spend our time crushing one another, competing and struggling toward the diminution of our abundance, in desperate search for the justification we can never create for ourselves, no matter how we try.

We find satisfaction in our work, joy and meaning, *but not salvation*. We dare not worship our work, but our work can become part of our worship of God.

Then we strive—not for our salvation, but that others can experience the grace we enjoy. We work energetically, enthusiastically, but not fearfully, frantically, or destructively. We live in relaxed acceptance of our ultimate worth, not needing to prove it, not anxious about it, not competing for it, but accepting our limitations, while we celebrate the eternity of love.

Our desire to achieve comes from the joy of self-expression, rather than the frantic pursuit of worth or the desperate fear of death. Our work finds its source in our desire to contribute, rather than the need to impress or overpower. An existential test of our significance is not our productivity. Rather, we enjoy the grace of God, the common grace of community, the grace of fruitful and productive lives.

Among Jesus' closing words on the cross were these: "It is finished." Our interpretation of these words depends upon our tone and inflection.

We can read them with the defeated tone of someone admitting surrender in a hopeless situation: "It's finished. I'm giving up. I can't go on."

Or we can read them as if a painter were adding the last brush stroke to a masterpiece, standing back to admire the completed canvas. Here "It is finished!" has the sound of victory.

For Jesus to say, "It is finished. It is complete," at the end of thirty-three years, redefines the meaning of a complete life. It is not the length of years—Jesus lived less than half of today's normal life span. A complete life is not defined by our accumulation of wealth, or because we are well known or have climbed to the top.

Complete and abundant life is a result of loving and being loved, becoming fully a person in relation to others, giving the best of ourselves, experiencing the exultation and anguish of living in faithful response to God's grace. Our highest ambitions are aimed beyond the horizon, to God's end and intention for all life.

The mystery of God's grace is deeper than we think. It washes away all lesser attainments. Of all God's creatures, only we are cursed with the consciousness of an unreturning past, and only we are privileged to contemplate the end and purpose of life—not just of our own lives or our work, but the end and purpose of life itself. Our perishable accomplishments find their meaning only as we derive it from the eternal presence and imperishable purposes of God. We are saved by grace.

"Thanks be to God, who gives us the victory through our Lord Jesus Christ. Therefore, my beloved, be steadfast, immovable, always excelling in the work of the Lord, because you know that in the Lord your labor is not in vain" (I Cor. 15:57-58).

Notes

CHAPTER 1. *Achievement and Appetite*

1. Quoted in Harry Emerson Fosdick, *On Being a Real Person* (New York: Harper & Row, 1943), p. 171.
2. Joseph Epstein, *Ambition: The Secret Passion* (Chicago: Ivan R. Dee, 1989/New York: E. P. Dutton, 1980), p. 1.
3. George Sweazey, "Should a Minister Be Ambitious?" The Princeton Seminary Tape Library (July 7, 1977).

CHAPTER 2. *Individualism and Competition*

1. Adele Faber and Elaine Mazlish, *Siblings Without Rivalry* (New York: Avon Books, 1987), p. 15.
2. David Elkind, *The Hurried Child* (Reading, Mass.: Addison-Wesley Publishing House, 1981), p. xii.
3. Dorothy Corkille Briggs, *Your Child's Self-Esteem* (Garden City, N. Y.: Doubleday, 1975), p. 85.
4. George Lakoff and Mark Johnson, *Metaphors We Live By* (University of Chicago Press, 1980), pp. 14-28.
5. Daniel D. Walker, *The Human Problems of the Minister* (New York: Harper & Brothers, 1960), p. 43.
6. Joseph Epstein, *Ambition: The Secret Passion* (Chicago: Ivan R. Dee, 1989/New York: E. P. Dutton, 1980), p. 13.
7. C. G. Jung, *Modern Man in Search of a Soul* (London: Routledge & Kegan Paul, 1981 / Dell & Baynes, 1933), p. 119.
8. Ernest Becker, *The Denial of Death* (New York: Macmillan Publishing Co., 1973), p. 152.
9. Ibid., p. 153.
10. Robert Bellah et al., *Habits of the Heart: Individualism and Commitment in American Life* (San Francisco: Harper & Row, 1985), pp. 150-51.

11. Tracy Kidder, *Among Schoolchildren* (New York: Avon Books, 1989), p. 87.
12. Epstein, *Ambition*, p. 1.
13. Becker, *Denial of Death,* p. 156.
14. Quoted in Epstein, *Ambition*, p. 273.
15. Becker, *Denial of Death*, p. ix.

CHAPTER 3. Ardent Desires and Deadly Appetites

1. This insight comes from Paul Jordan-Smith, "Seven (and More) Deadly Sins," *Parabola* (November 1985):42. See that issue for other articles on the seven deadly sins.
2. Ibid.
3. For discussions of pastoral infidelity and its dynamics, see Karen Lebacqz and Ronald G. Barton, *Sex in the Parish* (Louisville: Westminster/ John Knox Press, 1991) or Marie Fortune, *Is Nothing Sacred?* (San Francisco: Harper & Row, 1989).
4. Palmer J. Parker, *The Active Life: A Spirituality of Work, Creativity, and Caring* (San Francisco: Harper & Row, 1990), p. 2.

CHAPTER 4. Bodies and Bucks

1. Stephen R. Covey, *The Seven Habits of Highly Effective People* (New York: Simon & Schuster, 1989), p. 205.
2. John C. Harris, *Stress, Power, and Ministry* (Washington, D. C.: The Alban Institute, 1977), p. 100.

CHAPTER 5. Influence Peddlers

1. From a lecture by Joseph Allen. For a discussion of power in covenantal relationships, see Joseph Allen, *Love and Conflict: A Covenantal Model of Christian Ethics* (Nashville: Abingdon Press, 1984).
2. Keith Bridstone, *Church Politics* (New York: World Publishing Company, 1969), p. 86.
3. Frank G. Kirkpatrick, *Community: A Trinity of Models* (Washington, D. C.: Georgetown University Press, 1986), p. 168.

CHAPTER 6. Accountable and Complete

1. Frank G. Kirkpatrick, *Community: A Trinity of Models* (Washington, D. C.: Georgetown University Press, 1986), p. 187.
2. Dietrich Bonhoeffer, *Life Together: A Discussion of Christian Fellowship*, trans. John W. Doberstein (New York: Harper & Row, 1954), p. 20.
3. John C. Harris, *Stress, Power, and Ministry* (Washington, D. C.: The Alban Institute, 1977), see esp. pp. 56-57, 118-27.
4. Ibid., p. 125. "A healthy disenchantment" is Harris's phrase to describe the emotional distance pastors need to keep from their congregations for fuller engagement with them.

5. Recorded in David Tripp, *The Renewal of the Covenant in the Methodist Tradition* (London: Epworth Press, 1969), p. 183.

6. Carlyle Marney, *Priests to Each Other* (Valley Forge, Penna.: Judson Press, 1974), p. 45.

7. See Henri J. M. Nouwen, *In the Name of Jesus: Reflections on Christian Leadership* (New York: Crossroad Press, 1989), p. 16.